W9-CME-905

Practical Gemstone Craft

Practical Gemstone Craft

Helen Hutton

A Studio Book
The Viking Press
New York

Acknowledgements
The author would like to thank the following people: C. L. Forbes, M.A., Ph.D., Geology Department, Sedgwick Museum, University of Cambridge – for the Table of the origin of rocks, and for advice and assistance with the geological section of the book. Mr Norman Hughes, Geology Department, Sedgwick Museum, University of Cambridge – for advice, and assistance in the museum library. Mrs Mary Rose Clark, Lapidary, President of the Cambridge Lapidary Club – for technical advice and loan of material and equipment for photography. J. E. St Joseph, M.A., Ph.D., Department of Aerial Photography, University of Cambridge. Jim Ede, Kettle's Yard, Cambridge and Mrs C. Cobb, Cambridge – both of whom have loaned material and given assistance. Mrs John Hutton – for typing and checking the manuscript. Sam Carr, Batsford Ltd, London – for permission to reproduce material from my book *Mosaic Making*.

Drawings by Warwick Hutton

Published in 1972 by The Viking Press, Inc.
625 Madison Avenue, New York, N.Y. 10022

SBN 670–57061–3

Library of Congress catalog card number: 73-185385

Printed and bound in Great Britain

Contents

96394

Foreword

Minerals have long been sought after, both as specimens of individual beauty and as material to be transformed into fine jewels. There are many approaches to the subject of rocks and stones: they can be regarded simply as a form of investment; geologically, as the products of the great cycles of earth movements in our distant past; and as crystal structures which, with the aid of lapidary techniques, can be converted into objects of great beauty. This book keeps an excellent balance between these diverse aims.

Though the art of lapidary antedates recorded history and has spread all over the world, little is known of the techniques used by the lapidaries before the Christian era. One of the most primitive machines discovered was activated by a belt attached to a treadle. This method was used in China for centuries, and by means of this simple lathe, Chinese lapidaries have produced some of the finest jewelry the world has seen.

The diamond saw and electric furnace produced silicon and carbon, abrasives which have revolutionized the practical aspect of cutting and polishing stones to such an extent that this craft is now within the reach of the amateur.

One of the sad things that has happened to the lapidary craft, as with many others, is the division of processes between many people, i.e. cutters, faceters, doppers, sanders and polishers; so that nowadays the stone passes through many hands. But the amateur craftsman may still, like the lapidaries of ancient times, carry through the whole process himself, so enlarging and satisfying his love of stones.

We commend Mrs Hutton's comprehensive book to all who wish to begin and develop such interests, by studying the mineral kingdom; we feel that for them the book will be an invaluable source of information.

C. L. Forbes, M.A., Ph.D.
Department of Geology, Sedgwick Museum, University of Cambridge

Mrs Mary Rose Clark
President, Cambridge Lapidary Club, Cambridge

Glossary

Accessory minerals Minerals which are present in small amounts in any rock
Adamantine Impenetrably hard
Alluvial Materials which have been carried by flowing water
Amorphous Material which has no internal crystal structure
Asterism Star-like pattern in a mineral
Baroque Irregular in form
Basalt A fine-grained, dark, igneous rock
Botryoidal A globular mineral habit caused by a radial arrangement of crystals
Breccia Rock composed of angular or broken fragments
Cabochon Gem cut with a rounded or domed top
Carat Unit of weight for a gemstone
Carborundum Trade name for silicon carbide abrasive grit
Chalcedony The crypto-crystalline variety of silica
Chatoyancy Moving band of light across a mineral
Cleavage A line of weakness in crystalline substance causing it to separate more easily in one
    direction than another
Conchoidal Shell-like fracture in a rock or mineral
Conglomerate Rock composed of many pebbles cemented together
Crypto-crystalline A material which is composed of tightly packed sub-microscopic crystals
Cubic System Alternative name for Isometric system
Dendritic Habit Flattened tree-shaped growths of manganese or iron oxide in a stone
Dichroism Property due to double refraction in gemstones shown when different colours appear
    when they are viewed from several directions
Dopping The operation of attaching a stone to a handling rod with wax for manipulating it while
    grinding.
Double refraction Separation of light into two rays
Drusy Habit Clusters of tiny crystals
Extrusive Rocks Igneous rocks, usually from volcanic thrust, or volcanic rock that has solidified
Face Outer surface on a crystal
Facet Flat surface on a cut gem
Flats Tumbled stones, usually of softer varieties that have been worn flat due to faulty tumbling
Fluorescence Light given by a substance when exposed to visible radiation
Foliation Layered structure in metamorphic rock
Fibrous Fine thread-like structure
Fossil Remains or impression of ancient animal or plant
Fracture Irregular breakage of mineral or rock
Geode A rounded rock mass, usually hollow and crystal lined
Gneiss A coarse grained metamorphic rock, with contrasting banding
Granite A coarse-grained igneous rock usually composed of quartz, feldspar and mica
Habit Shape or crystal form assumed by a mineral
Hardness Scale Resistance of a mineral to being scratched. Mohs' Scale is used throughout the
    book
Hoppers Tumbling barrels

Hornfelsed   Rocks which have been strongly altered by the intrusion of hot magma, often partly re-crystallized.

Hypabyssal   Igneous rocks of medium texture, sometimes porphyritic that crystallize fairly quickly at no great depth. Occurring in minor inclusions such as dykes and sills

Igneous   Rocks deriving from volcanic sources or lava

Impurities   Small amount of foreign elements in a mineral

Inclusions   Fragments or particles of another mineral enclosed within a rock or crystal

Intrusive   Igneous rock below the surface

Isometric   One of the six crystal systems

Lap   A horizontal revolving circular disc covered with leather, wood or soft metal for polishing gemstones

Lapidary   A person working with gems or stones and the art of working with gems and stones

Lava   Molten rock on the surface

Lustre   The result of reflected light on a mineral

Magma   Molten material from which igneous rocks are formed

Mammillary   Smooth rounded rock masses, resembling breasts. Malachite occur in this form

Massive form   Material not occurring in discernible individual crystals. Usually in large portions

Matrix   Main body of rock in which crystals, fossils or other minerals are embedded

Metamorphic   Rock or mineral which has been extensively changed

Mineral   Chemical compounds of definite composition found as constituents of rocks

Mohs' Scale   Scale of hardness used for minerals

Nacre   Iridescent shell layer of pearl mollusc

Nodule   A geode that is completely filled and solid

Oolitic   Limestone variety containing spherical particles of calcium carbonate

Opalised   Converted from original form to include silica

Opalescence   The milky or pearly reflections from the interior of a gemstone

Orbicular   Containing round or spherical inclusions

Orthorhombic   One of the six crystal systems

Pegmatite   Coarse granite rocks which have cooled slowly allowing the formation of large, well-formed gem crystals

Petrified wood   Wood which has had its original structure replaced by silica, leaving original formation visible

Pleochroism   An optical property relating to colour refraction

Porphyritic   Texture of igneous rock containing large crystals set in finer ground mass

Prismatic   Pencil-shaped mineral

R.P.M.   Revolutions per minute. The turning speed of a machine

Schist   A rock and mineral compressed into thin layers by metamorphic action

Sedimentary   A rock formed from sediments or from material once in solution

Shale   A rock formed from mud

Slabbing   The act of sawing rocks into slabs or slices

Silica   Dioxide of silicon, occurring in crystalline form as quartz

Specific gravity   Relative weight of a substance compared to water

Striations   Closely placed fine parallel lines

Streak   Colour of a mineral when powdered

Tabular Habit   Flattish book-shaped mineral deposit

Tin Oxide   Powder for polishing gemstones and pebbles

Tetragonal   One of the six crystal systems

Thunder Egg   A rounded or ovoid body containing agate or opal

Translucent   Allowing the passage of light but not permitting a clear view of any object

Triclinic   One of the six crystal systems

Texture   Size, shape and patterns of grains in a rock

Vein   A seam or small crack in a rock, usually lined with crystalline incrustations

Vitreous   Glassy surface reflection on a mineral

Undercutting   Usually occurring in gemstones of two or more minerals of differing properties, causing weaker portions to wear away at a faster rate under abrasive processes

Introduction

This book sets out to cover the general interests of the lapidary, and, with this in mind, to create a balance between the geological background of minerals, descriptions of them, and techniques for cutting and polishing them.

Collecting, polishing, setting and displaying all have an irresistible fascination when an interest in lapidary has been aroused. Travel, holidays, and even short seaside expeditions become exciting pilgrimages of discovery.

In selecting material to describe in chapter 4, it has not been possible to include all those minerals which appear in the lists of lapidary dealers. This is partly because some stones (such as agates) occur in innumerable varieties; and partly because techniques requiring more advanced skills have been omitted. The precious gemstones – diamond, ruby, sapphire and some others – have thus been excluded, as they require professional faceting.

Rarity and cost rule out some precious stones for the amateur lapidary and collector, but excellent 'rough' (i.e. untreated) material is available from suppliers. Most of the world's areas of rich mineral deposits are now commercially owned and not available to the general public, but there are still some parts accessible to everyone. Ordinary rocks and stones may have a beauty not unlike the glowing colour of a gem, but of a more subtle quality – recognizable to the eye of the artist; or to the eye seeking distinction of form and shape, texture, tone and pattern. They have a further quality recognized by the hand – tactility.

Certain stones, often the ovoid ones, smooth or granular to the touch, have the beauty of a piece of sculpture, the purity of which would be destroyed by polishing or re-shaping the essential form. It is worth learning to recognize these stones when you come upon them, and preserve their character intact. An example of such stones occurs near Hartland Point, on the west coast of England, in the form of oval boulders of dark grey sandstone, ringed with pencil-thin circles of white quartz. They lie huddled in vast throngs beneath the cliffs, worn to a sculptural smoothness by the pounding sea. See figs 1 and 2 for photographs of these stones.

Fig 1 Large sandstone boulders showing quartz veining. Photo author

Fig 2 Sandstone boulders in garden sink. Photo author

Further examples of nature's ingenuity of design are found in the rhythmical foliations of gneiss (fig. 3) and schist (fig. 4), and the fine-banded arrangements of many other common stones, seen at their best along the tideline while gleaming wet.

An important preliminary for the collector is to make full use of the regional and national geology museums. Wherever there are mineral deposits of any significance, there are regional museums, with information, maps, lectures and general advice. National museums display a comprehensive collection of rocks and minerals, and general advice and lectures are available. They also sell booklets and colour slides of the more common minerals, which are a considerable help in identification.

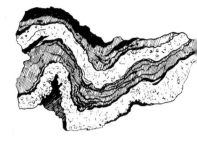

Fig 3 Folded gneiss

It is impressive to see outstanding examples of minerals, perhaps some found locally; also magnificent specimens from abroad, scintillating in their cases. Sometimes one visits a museum to check and compare data on a recent find, at other times the purpose may be more general, but it is always a foray into the magic world of Aladdin's cave.

Indications of some well-known localities of gems in England have been included in the map on page 192. It is impossible to give up-to-date information as to accessibility and availability of sites, and the local geology museum or geological survey maps should be consulted. In the United States most states produce Gem Trail maps.

Even when material is bought direct from a lapidary dealer, it is worthwhile having some understanding of the characteristics and qualities of the stones. Although many are described in chapter 2, a museum can often be of more use than a text book.

Fig 4 Mica schist

Lapidary clubs are becoming very numerous, and provide an opportunity to use equipment and practise skills, as well as discussions on technical problems, mineral identification sessions, and 'rock-swaps'. The joint purchase of machinery makes it possible for everyone to learn to use lapidary equipment. There are organized expeditions to museums, and to beaches and sites of mineral deposits.

Finally it should be recognized that every part of the world provides some hunting ground for gemstone material, some considerably richer than others. The sources appear to be unending, and new finds are frequently uncovered.

Lapidary can become an obsession – carried out as a simple and inexpensive hobby or as a complex art form.

1 The nature of rocks and minerals

The earth's crust, which is several miles thick, is composed of rocks. All these rocks are interesting to the lapidary, and it is an advantage to be familiar with their origin and properties.

A rock is an aggregate of mineral grains, and is often composed of quite a number of minerals. Granite, which is a rock, is largely made up of three minerals: quartz, feldspar and mica, the crystals of which are large enough to be distinguishable by the naked eye.

A mineral, on the other hand, is a substance forming part of the earth's crust which has a more or less definite chemical composition and physical characteristics by which it may be recognized wherever it is found. To take an example, quartz, a mineral important to the lapidary, is composed of one atom of silicon to every two atoms of oxygen.

Its chemical formula is SiO_2, and it may always be recognized by its crystal system, hardness, lustre, fracture and the various other properties which will be described later in this chapter.

There are three main groups of rocks.

1 IGNEOUS

These are varied in age, and are believed to have come from molten material deep below the earth's surface. Hence the name 'igneous', which means 'fiery'. There are two classes of igneous rocks – volcanic (extrusive) and plutonic (intrusive).

Volcanic rocks have been forced upwards while still in a molten state, pouring through fissures and volcanic vents to spread out in lava flows, or to build up as heaps of fragments. Generally speaking, cooling has been rapid, and their mineral content has had no time to form large crystals, so rocks of this type are fine-grained or glassy. Obsidian of a fine glassy nature, and basalt of a fine-grained mass of small crystals are examples of this class.

Intrusive rocks are those which are thought to have cooled more slowly beneath the earth's surface, solidifying gradually, and thus allowing the individual crystals to grow to large sizes. Granite shows its crystals of individual minerals plainly. Porphyritic textures, which are large, well-formed crystals (due to slow cooling) embedded in a finer ground mass, are either extrusive or intrusive.

2 SEDIMENTARY

This second major group (the name of which is self-explanatory), is composed of fragments of pre-existing rocks which have been broken, often altered chemically, and carried by various agents (wind, rain, rivers and tides), to new places to form deposits. These rocks form in layers or strata (fig. 6).

Sediments often contain the remains of living things many millions of years old in the form of fossils. These frequently represent plants and animals of extinct types.

Limestone is of sedimentary origin. It is often composed of countless minute fossils which merge into a mosaic, and can be polished very successfully. Shales and sandstones – with their stratified layers – and conglomerates (which look like plum puddings), are further examples of sedimentary deposits.

Fig 5   Igneous rock structure (columnar formation) at Ailsa Craig, Ayr. Courtesy Dr J. K. St Joseph, Cambridge University Collection

Fig 6 Sedimentary rock structure at St Bee's Head, Cumberland. Courtesy Dr J. L. St Joseph, Cambridge University Collection

The outstanding features to remember about sedimentary rocks are firstly that they are normally stratified or bedded, and occur in layers parallel to the surface on which they were deposited. Secondly that they are made up of fragments of pre-existing rocks, minerals and fossils, which are sometimes clearly visible (as in conglomerates, which are composed of various pebbles cemented together in a matrix of some tough binding mineral).

Sedimentary rocks, with the exception of limestone, are generally poor material for gemstones and lapidary as they are fairly soft, but when slabbed and polished some of their interestingly-textured patterns are enchanting.

3 METAMORPHIC

This is a group of rocks of igneous or sedimentary origin which have undergone changes (metamorphism) from their initial form. Such changes are due to heat, or to high pressure causing chemical interaction, or to some combination of these factors. The rocks are changed from their original textures and minerals to different types altogether (figs 8 and 9). In fact, over the geological ages, a rock may be changed more than once. Fossils are destroyed during metamorphism. Regions hundreds of miles in extent and several miles in thickness have been subjected to great pressure and intense folding. New materials are formed, often occurring in layers, such as schist and gneiss. An example of metamorphism is the re-crystallization of limestone into marble (see Table of the origin of rocks, fig. 7). Mud, subjected to pressure, is first hardened to slate and may be cleaved into the typical thin sheets. Even more intense heat and pressure will result in the further development of mica-like minerals, so that the original mud finally emerges as a schist.

Study the Table of the origin of rocks below.

Identification of minerals

One must appreciate the various properties and characteristics of minerals in order to bring to life their finest qualities. There is frequently a be-wildering difference of colour occurring in the same species, while diverse stones sometimes resemble each other quite closely. Identification can be difficult without guidelines.

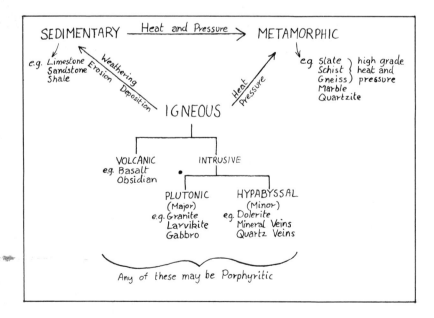

Fig 7 Table of the origin of rocks. Courtesy Dr C. L. Forbes, Geology Department, University of Cambridge

Fig 8 Metamorphic rock structure at Welcombe Mouth, Devon. Sediments tilted from the original horizontal. Photo author

Fig 9 Metamorphic rock structure, showing quartz veining, at Welcombe Mouth, Devon. Photo author

Some of the properties of gemstones are (1) crystalline system and (2) habit, (3) hardness, (4) cleavage and fracture; and some of the optical properties, including lustre, transparency or opacity, pleochroism (dichroism and trichroism), chatoyancy and asterism. Specific gravity is given in a table on p. 91. Most of the optical properties will only be briefly defined (see p. 20).

1 CRYSTAL SYSTEMS

The majority of minerals occur in definite forms, according to the crystal system dictated by their particular atomic pattern. The crystals are bounded by series of planes known as 'sets of faces'. There are seven systems: cubic (or isometric), tetragonal, orthorhombic, hexagonal, trigonal, monoclinic and triclinic (see fig. 10).

Some crystals are so perfect in their beauty and symmetry that it is hard to believe that they are formed naturally. Others show distortions and inclusions which reveal some interruption in their development. Twin crystals and clusters are quite common. Typical examples of the trigonal system are quartz, tourmaline, and calcite; while the hexagonal system includes apatite and beryl.

Fig. 10 shows the crystal systems and some of the minerals common to each.

Fig 10 Crystal systems:

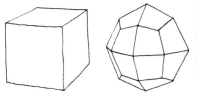

1 Cubic   garnet

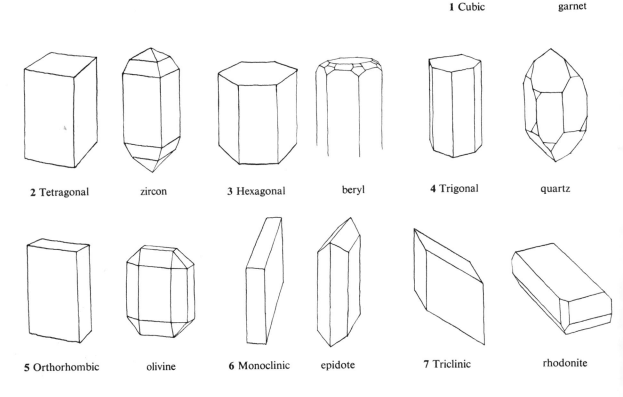

2 Tetragonal   zircon   **3** Hexagonal   beryl   **4** Trigonal   quartz

5 Orthorhombic   olivine   **6** Monoclinic   epidote   **7** Triclinic   rhodonite

Fig 11 Crystal habit: arborescent

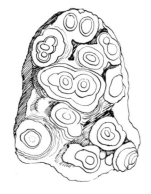

Fig 12 Crystal habit: mamillary

2 CRYSTAL HABIT

Crystals tend to develop in particular ways, and recognition of characteristic habits helps to identify them. Tabular habit suggests a table-top or a book, appearing in thin, rectangular shapes. Arborescent (fig. 11) or dendritic crystals branch out in the likeness of a tree or fern. The mammilary habit (fig. 12) taken by malachite is strikingly reminiscent of breast-like shapes. Other descriptive habits are botryoidal (grape-like); fibrous; filiform, reticulated and drusy (this last is common in quartz, when the surface is covered with tiny crystals, giving the typical sparkle). Drusy cavities are often found in geodes – an infilling of a rock cavity, often a steam bubble in lava. A druse is an actual cavity in a rock, lined with the same sort of crystals as form the surrounding rock.

3 HARDNESS

Hardness is a very useful guide for mineral identification. It is necessary to know the hardness of a gemstone both for cutting and for polishing – also for tumbling, because if hard and soft stones are polished together in a tumbler, the result may well be disastrous, the softer stones being partially or entirely ground away.

Mohs' Scale of Hardness, which is the one most commonly used, consists of ten standard minerals arranged in order so that each will scratch those occurring before it, but will in turn be scratched by those after it.

Starting with the softest, the scale is as follows:

1 Talc
2 Gypsum
3 Calcite
4 Fluorite
5 Apatite
6 Orthoclase, feldspar
7 Quartz
8 Topaz
9 Corundum
10 Diamond

A point to note, however, is that the intervals in Mohs' Scale are not of equal value. Diamond is so much harder than any other mineral that the difference between it and corundum is much greater than that between any other minerals on the scale. A simple test is as follows: Hardness $2\frac{1}{2}$ can be scratched by a fingernail; Hardness 4 by a copper coin; Hardness $5\frac{1}{2}$ by a penknife; Hardness $6\frac{1}{2}$ by a steel file. Gauges to test hardness may be bought from lapidary suppliers.

Although some minerals are quite soft, they more than compensate for it by their degree of toughness. Jade, for example, is comparatively soft (Hardness 6 to $6\frac{1}{2}$), but its densely-felted texture of interlocked crystals gives it a strength that enables it to be cut in very thin slices without fear of breaking.

4 CLEAVAGE AND FRACTURE

Cleavage refers to the way in which crystals, when stressed, tend to split only in certain directions. The direction depends on the atomic arrangement. Though not all minerals exhibit cleavage, it is of great importance in the process of cutting and polishing gemstones. See figs 13, 14.

Fracture refers to ordinary breaking. All stones are sufficiently brittle to be fractured by a fairly violent blow. Stones differ in the way they break, depending on their mineral structure. Obsidian and quartz break smoothly, with shell-like convexities and concavities (conchoidal fracture, fig. 15), other rocks and minerals fracture unevenly.

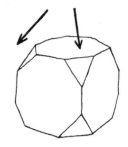

Fig 13 Cleavage: octahedral

Fig 14 Cleavage: rhombohedral

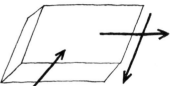

Optical properties

COLOUR

This should be used with caution as a means of identifying minerals. It is often misleading, as the tinge in a gemstone may be caused by impurities. Other optical properties that should help towards identification are brilliancy, fire, iridescence (as in the opal), and varying degrees of transparency and translucency.

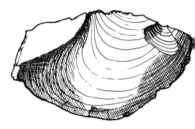

Fig 15 Fracture: conchoidal (eg flint)

LUSTRE

This is the term used to describe the surface effect of reflection and refraction which occurs when light strikes a bright surface. The words commonly used to describe the type of lustre are: metallic (occurring chiefly in ores), adamantine (as in diamonds), vitreous (glassy, as in quartz and many gemstones), resinous (as in some kinds of garnet or amber), silky (as in satin spar and cat's eye), pearly (as in moonstones), waxy (as in topaz).

REFRACTION, PLEOCHROISM, CHATOYANCY and ASTERISM

These will be commented on very briefly since, although interesting and important, they are mainly of relevance to the faceting of gemstones.

Refraction When the light from outside strikes the surface of a transparent body, some of it is reflected and some penetrates the substance. The light in the latter case does not follow the original course but is bent, 'refracted', and proceeds in a new direction.

Pleochroism (dichroism, trichroism) This is a phenomenon occurring only in coloured, doubly-refractive gemstones, and results in the gem appearing in different colours according to the direction of view. Green tourmaline shows the two-colour effect of dichroism very markedly. Alexandrite shows three colours (trichroism).

Chatoyancy and asterism This is the effect, best seen in the cat's eye, of a silky sheen. It is the result of bundles of fine linear inclusions (thread-like lines) lying parallel, so that when the stone is viewed at right-angles a band of light is seen running across the bundles. Many translucent minerals sufficiently fibrous in structure will show chatoyancy if suitably cut. Cabochons reveal this to its best advantage, and must be cut with the fibres lying flat, and parallel to the base of the stone. Chrysoberyl and many other translucent minerals, such as tourmaline and beryl, will show chatoyancy when this method of cutting is followed. Sometimes the linear inclusions occur in several directions, giving a star-like effect, known as asterism. This is seen in the ruby, sapphire, aquamarine, garnet and others.

This is the full extent of the properties of gemstones to be examined in this section, but it seems wrong to end without a brief comment on the mineral which is both popular and useful in lapidary work – quartz.

Quartz

This is one of the hardest and most stable of the minerals, so that it occurs abundantly in many rocks of varying origin. It readily takes a good polish.

Quartz is found in every part of the world, the two general varieties being large crystals with well-defined habits, and the massive form, composed of minute grains or fibres too small to be distinguishable. The first sort is mainly transparent and is known as 'crystalline' (coarse crystals), while the second is translucent to opaque and is termed 'crypto-crystalline'. Both are crystalline quartz, differing only in appearance caused by habit of growth.

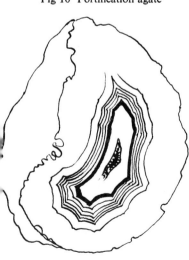

Fig 16 Fortification agate

An impressive type of crypto-crystalline quartz is agate (fig. 16). Agates are widely distributed, as are the other quartz minerals, being found in every part of the world, although in some localities they are much more abundant.

They are frequently found in the form of geodes. These are pitted balls, easily separated from the enclosing rock. They give little indication of their exciting interior, which is often lined with fine crystals.

The thunder egg, a special type of agate nodule, occurring widely in Oregon, North America, differs from other geodes in that the centre is filled with solid agate. It is described in more detail in chapter 3.

Countless other rocks and minerals are of interest to the collector, and those which are unsuitable for use as gemstones may often be slabbed and polished. Others may attract attention by their shape alone. Flints with holes in them may contain little pebbles within the cavity. These may be collected for their interesting forms, and are especially fascinating when tumble-polished.

Where specimens may be found

PEGMATITES

These are coarse-grained veins, usually running through granite outcrops in the form of bodies of rock, seldom more than a mile long but often very deep. Within these veins large crystals occur in the irregular fabric when favourable conditions exist.

There are no very spectacular pegmatites in Britain, although some interesting ones occur in the Cairngorm Mountains in Scotland, containing golden-brown quartz in pegmatite veins in granite. Crystals of dramatic proportions have been found in pegmatites of North America and Brazil. The largest recorded crystals have, in fact, come from pegmatites. The finest quartz crystal ever recorded, weighing over five tons, was found in a Brazilian pegmatite, while others of enormous proportions have occurred in the Ural Mountains, South West Africa, Tanzania, Sweden, Finland, Norway and Germany. The Black Hills of South Dakota (Etta Mines) produce huge spodumene 'logs' sticking up in a matrix of feldspar – an eerie sight – and a beryl crystal weighing a hundred tons has been reported from another mine there.

VUGS

These are druses found in pegmatites and mineral veins, and fine crystals are often discovered lining the cavity. In each such treasure-house, perfectly developed crystals of several gem species may be revealed.

OTHER LOCALITIES

In North America, gem localities are listed extensively, state by state, and mineral survey maps can be obtained for each area. Many state-owned and privately-owned sites require that you first obtain a permit to collect, and sometimes a small fee must be paid.

Fig 17 Serpentine

There are still many areas where the collector may roam at will, although certain sorts of places are more favourable than others, and it is to these that you must direct your attention.

Beaches and rivers generally yield several different minerals, which have come from many sources. These are in the form of pebbles, usually the more common varieties – such as sandstone, granite, flint, dolerite, chert, schist, gneiss, gabbro, conglomerate (fig. 18), breccia and quartzite. On certain favoured stretches, however, serpentine (fig. 17), jasper, carnelian, agate, chaledony, quartz, amber and jet may be found.

Fig 18 Conglomerate of flint pebbles

Hot springs and thermal regions are another likely place to look. Even if the springs themselves are defunct, interesting deposits should be in evidence.

Mines, quarries and gravel pits may yield specimens, sometimes in the form of really worthwhile crystals. Permission to enter must be obtained, of course, as there may well be some danger.

Fig 19 Oolitic limestone

The vast road-building programmes in progress in most countries, cutting through mountains and rising across valleys, bring to light many rocks of great interest to the collector. Landslides are also good hunting grounds, but may be dangerous.

Ornamental stones for slabbing – marble, serpentine, oolitic limestone (fig. 19), laurvikite, porphyritic granites and many others – can usually be had in small pieces discarded by monumental masons.

A locality section in comprehensive detail is not possible in this book, but in the England Localities Map at the end (p. 92), some of the more well-known areas of mineral deposits are discussed and marked.

One of the best ways to learn about collecting is to accompany an organized field trip to a well-known locality. Lapidary and geology clubs arrange such expeditions and you may have the additional bonus of experienced companions.

2 Rocks and pebbles for collecting and tumbling

The majority of the stones and pebbles described in this section may be found on most beaches, although certain stretches of coastline may be especially noted for specific varieties. For instance, the area of the Lizard, on the south west coast of England, is unrivalled for its superb serpentine; while carnelians of brilliant tints are common on the north coast of Norfolk (fig. 29) – for those with sharp eyes!

It is important to check tide times, as your chosen stretch of coast may be inaccessible at high tide, or your retreat cut off.

Other stones and pebbles may be sought at the mouths of rivers and in gravel beds and pits – for example, large varieties of agate, jasper and chalcedony are to be found in the gravel of the Rio Grande River in Texas. Water-worn beach and river-bed pebbles are fine tumbling material. Larger material, in the form of rocks, are better broken with a hammer and chisel into reasonably-sized pieces before tumbling.

Breccia and conglomerate

Both these are of sedimentary origin, composed of a concreted mass of debris. The fragments forming breccia are highly angular. This is because they have not been transported for any distance, and therefore have not had the chance to rub against each other and become rounded. Consequently the sizing and shaping are irregular and poorly sorted.

Conglomerate is a well-sorted, rounded and cross-bedded stone, sectionally like a slice of plum pudding. It is in fact commonly known as 'pudding stone'. Fossil conglomerates (fig. 20) are common, and both these and breccia are often embedded with tiny crystals of distinctive patterns. They make fine tumbling material.

Granite

An igneous rock of intrusive origin, granite is common and very widespread. Its varied tones of reds and greys, its coarse and fine textures, often scintillating with mica flakes, make it a distinctive rock. Cornish granite,

Fig 20 Large polished decorative
stones, showing fossil conglomerate

a well-known type which extends over great areas of the Cornish peninsula,
is a mixture of quartz, white feldspar and sparkling black mica flecks.
Pebbles are common, and although very hard, granite tumble-polishes
well with material of equal hardness. Porphyritic granite is outstandingly
decorative.

Gneiss and schist

Both are sparkling glittering rocks (especially when wet). They are highly
crystalline.

Gneiss is generally streaked or banded, composed of metamorphosed

granite or intrusive rock of similar composition. It has a layered arrangement of minute crystals of quartz, mica and feldspar of very arresting pattern.

Schist has innumerable cleavage planes and can be split into fine layers – it is easily recognized by the very clear foliations in parallel alignment. 'Schist' is of Greek derivation, the word meaning 'easily split'. The banding is narrower than in gneiss and more finely grained, but the same shimmering lustre is there, although the composition is now only quartz and mica.

Both these rocks are easily identifiable from rocks of sedimentary origin by their flakiness. They are too soft to be suitable for tumble-polishing, but if tumbled by themselves and allowed a rather longer polishing time, some varieties give good results (figs 3, 4)

Fig 21 Tumbled decorative stones

Sandstone

These stones are of sedimentary origin, composed entirely of sand grains which have been deposited at the bottom of the sea, in the beds of lakes, or on the land. The nature of the grains gives an indication as to the manner in which the original rock was formed. Various cementing materials bind the grains together. The reddish-brown sandstones are bound with an iron material; others are cemented with quartz; while the green variety is bound with a mineral called glauconite. These stones vary considerably in their degree of hardness, this also being affected by the binding material, which varies greatly. The texture may be coarse or fine-grained. Sandstone, especially sandstone pebbles, is abundant in every country and can be tumble-polished successfully.

Gabbro and dolerite

Intrusive, igneous rocks, dark grey in colour, with mineral crystals deeply intermeshed, making them very tough and heavy. The texture of dolerite is rather more fine-grained than gabbro, and generally a lighter grey. Both are plentiful in pebble form, and make good tumbling material, bearing in mind that they are very hard.

Slate

This sedimentary rock was originally shale (formed from mud) but has undergone terrific pressure from movements of the earth's crust, which cause the layered cleavage planes. It is found in mountainous areas, and is of a grey-green to a reddish-purple in colour, flakes of mica giving it the characteristic sheen. It may be tumbled, but is very soft.

Quartzite

This is metamorphosed sandstone, the quartz grains having re-crystallized to form an interlocking mosaic, which makes the rock compact and lustrous, also very hard and tough. The colour is variable, depending on the mineral staining, and may be streaked or mottled in shades of brown, purplish blue or blue. It is to be found on beaches, stream beds and gravel pits. Quartzite makes good polishing material, but for best results tumble separately.

Laurvikite

This is a Norwegian rock, having travelled across the North Sea in ice sheets. It is also found on the coasts of Yorkshire, and pebbles of it may be found in the boulder-clays of the east coast of England. Typically it is blackish in colour, with flashes of blue when viewed from different angles. A very striking stone when polished in slabs or tumbled.

Limestone

A sedimentary rock, variable in colour, texture and origin. Many fossilized animals and marine life contribute the minerals that form the different varieties. Oolitic limestone consists of a mass of tiny concretions that build up around a small nucleus, resulting in tiny spheres. This is a very impressive form of limestone, and is quite common in pebble form. Crystalline and shell limestone are two other varieties. An identification test is its solubility in dilute hydrochloric acid, and its weathering in humid climates. It is rather soft for tumbling, but may be slabbed and polished. Of varying softness, depending on variety and composition.

Marble

A metamorphic rock, re-crystallized from limestone to form a granular mosaic of interesting texture. Normally white, but often tinted by various minerals to shades of yellow, green, brown and black, frequently veined. Although only of Hardness 3, it is compact and polishes well. Tumble as for serpentine.

3 Quartz and its varieties

The importance of quartz has already been mentioned in chapter 1. Its many varieties have the same identifying features, with individual characteristics which will be described under the name of each type. The composition is silicon dioxide, which is the most widespread mineral in nature, making up many granite igneous rocks, and always recognizable by its glassy appearance.

Crystal system trigonal. *Crystal habit* well-formed prismatic crystals, usually in sets of three, capped with pyramids. Also in massive granular form. *Hardness* 7. *Cleavage* none. *Lustre* vitreous. Double refraction. Some varieties exhibit dichroism.

Transparent varieties

ROCK CRYSTAL
Clear, colourless quartz, found in crystals varying in size from a tiny speck to a yard or more in length. Distinguishable by its low specific gravity and lack of fire. Very widespread. Cheap.

AMETHYST
Although a precious stone which should be faceted, it is actually purple quartz (fig. 34). The colour varies considerably in depth and affects its value. The gem variety is expensive, while amethystine quartz is fairly cheap. Birthstone for March.

CITRINE
A clear yellow quartz of gem quality, varying greatly in depth of colour – the richest in depth being the most expensive. Generally fairly expensive.

SMOKY QUARTZ
The colour range is from shades of pale smoky brown to a deep brown. The Scottish variety, known as cairngorm, is a golden brown. Shows dichroism in the deeper-coloured specimens. Rough smoky quartz is sold fairly cheaply by the pound.

ROSE QUARTZ

As the name suggests, this is a rose red or delicate pink, rarely showing crystal faces (fig. 32). It is often flawed and cracked. The pinkish tinge is due to manganese, and is liable to fade in bright sunlight. The best rose quartz comes from Brazil. Makes fine cabochons. Do not tumble with agate or jasper. Medium-priced to expensive, depending on quality and locality.

RUTILATED QUARTZ

This beautiful variety is crystal clear, with yellowish to red-brown inclusions arrayed in myriads of bright, sparkling needles of rutile, which flash in all directions. Rutile is also found in other quartzes. Rutilated quartz makes fine cabochons and is medium-priced to expensive, depending on quality.

MILKY QUARTZ

Hazy and semi-opaque in structure, resembling milk. A rather common variety, also known as vein-quartz, it is often dyed and is cheap to buy.

AVENTURINE QUARTZ

Enclosed discs of mica, haematite, or other flaky minerals give a peculiar gold-spangled appearance to the reflected light when this variety is polished. Tumble alone, or only with rose quartz, rock crystal, amethystine quartz. Chips for tumbling are medium-priced.

TOURMALINATED QUARTZ

Similar to smoky quartz, this variety contains inclusions of black tourmaline, usually as coarse needles. It can appear as a handsome stone when cut and well polished. Rather expensive when available.

QUARTZ CAT'S EYE AND TIGER EYE

In this type of quartz, the presence of parallel fibres of asbestos gives the effect of a luminous banding, which is best seen when the stone is cabochon-cut. Tiger eye is a fibrous quartz, golden-yellow in colour. When cut and polished it gives a fine chatoyant effect. It is found in schist-quartz. Medium-priced.

Crypto-crystalline, translucent and opaque

These varieties of chalcedony have no external crystalline form, and seem to be quite amorphous. Actually they have a fibrous structure, are doubly refracting and crystalline, when viewed microscopically. Agates are the commonest and the most interesting in this group, and are worth a study in themselves.

In this form of chalcedony the familiar concentric or banded appearance is due to the cavity in which the agate is formed. The many varieties are generally named according to their pattern or banding, although others are named after their place of origin. Colours are very varied and intermingled, and dyeing is very common. The clear layers of chalcedony being rather porous, they will absorb colouring matter, while the whitish opaline bands are impervious to it. Although some consider the natural banding of the agate of more subtle colouring, the more vivid colours when dyed bring out the zonal structure of the stone.

Crystal system amorphous (to the naked eye). *Crystal habit* occurs in massive mammillary or botryoidal form, sometimes stalactitic. *Hardness* 6½ to 7. *Cleavage* none. *Fracture* conchoidal. *Lustre* vitreous, to dull or waxy.

Varieties

COMMON CHALCEDONY

In its ordinary form chalcedony is bluish to greyish in colour. It is very widespread in most countries, but, owing to its rather dull appearance, is not as popular as the more colourful varieties. It is very tough, and cheap.

CARNELIAN

The translucent variety is found in shades of pale to deep yellow, reddish brown, clear red, and a brilliant bright orange which is prized by collectors. Seashore pebbles may be detected at low tide by their glowing colours, like illuminations among the grey mass of shingle. They are the birthstone for July. May be bought fairly cheaply when available.

CHRYSOPRASE

A variety coloured green by a compound of nickel oxides. It is the birthstone for May. It is sometimes difficult to polish, tending to undercut.

JASPER (BLOODSTONE OR HELIOTROPE)

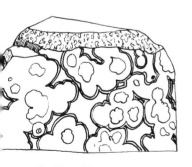

Fig 22 Orbicular jasper

An opaque, massive and compact variety, impregnated with impurities which give red, yellow or brown flecks. In ribbon jasper, the colours run in stripes and zones. The bloodstone variety is dark green chalcedony flecked with red, and at one time was worn in an amulet in the belief that it would stop bleeding. The stone is very decorative and rewarding to polish. Orbicular jasper (fig. 22) is another beautiful variety. Occurrences are widespread, and it is cheap to buy from suppliers.

ONYX AND SARDONYX

Straight-banded chalcedony in strongly contrasting colours. Sard or carnelian are included in the banding in sardonyx. Very effective as cabochons, and comparatively cheap to buy.

PETRIFIED WOOD (opalized and agatized)
The organic remains of wood, coral, bone are replaced by chalcedony, agate or jasper in this decorative form (fig. 23). When tumbling, an additional coarse grind may be needed to polish this material successfully. US varieties cheap.

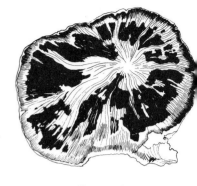
Fig 23 Petrified wood

FLINT AND CHERT
Grey or blackish amorphous material, which has a dull, waxy lustre. Very hard and weather-resistant. Often found in unusual, irregular shapes, which make interesting specimens for collections. Chert fossil agates have good patterns. Cheap.

AGATE VARIETIES
This is a form of chalcedony, with the familiar concentric-banded appearance, the cause of which must be explained. Volcanic action caused gas pockets in volcanic ash, and at a later stage these were filled by cold silica, into which filtered minerals of various colours, which eventually solidified. An interesting variety known as orbicular (eye) agate is illustrated in fig. 24. Other impressive forms of agate are the geode and the thunder egg mentioned in chapter 1.

Fortification Banding, often multi-coloured, taking angular turns like the aerial view of an old fortress. Commercial material is nearly always dyed. Often occurs with crystals in the centre. Cheap to medium price, depending on quality.

Fig 24 Orbicular agate

Moss Translucent chalcedony with inclusions of any colour (though more frequently green) arranged in moss-like, tree-like or flower-like patterns (fig. 26). A rather beautiful variety, of cheap to medium price.

Banded (or riband) Colours arranged in parallel bands, often wavy. Commercial material is usually dyed or altered in colour by heat treatment. Fairly cheap.

Iris (or rainbow) Banded, showing all the colours of the spectrum when sliced thinly. Fairly cheap.

Ruin Sometimes known as 'brecciated'. Patterns resembling the outline of ruins. The straight bands are shattered and arranged in angular patterns. Rather rare. Prices variable.

Plume A type of moss agate, with inclusions looking like waving ostrich feathers. An especially beautiful variety is found in Oregon, US – clear agate with delicate lace-like plumes. Prized by collectors. Medium-priced.

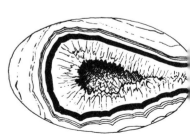
Fig 25 Agate geode

Sagenite More commonly known as rutilated quartz. Clear chalcedony containing tiny needle inclusions of foreign minerals. Medium-priced.

Fig 26 Moss agate

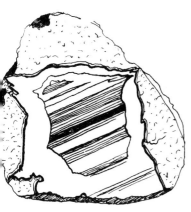

Fig 27 Section of thunder egg

Crazy lace   Natural colouring with lacy patterns. Medium-priced.

Turritella   Petrified mollusc shells in dark agate. Very dark varieties should be called turritella jasper. Very decorative. Medium-priced.

Landscape   Usually white or grey chalcedony with inclusions of manganese oxide, which form fanciful landscapes – sometimes strangely realistic. Medium-priced.

Many other varieties exist which are named after their locality of origin. These are Montana, Uruguayan, Brazilian, Mexican, Idar Oberstein (no longer available), Australian.

Further impressive variations of the chalcedony family are desert roses, geodes, nodules and thunder eggs.

DESERT ROSES

Desert rose is properly the term used to describe a habit of barite, but the flattened rose-like form of chalcedony, shaped as a brownish-pink nodule, is the well-known desert rose sought by collectors. These resemble oyster shells, are translucent to opaque, and some have brown spots.

Carefully ground, they reveal opalescent flashes of colour and have been called fire agates. Cutting and polishing require some skill.

GEODES

Usually hollow balls of mineralized earth, into which ground waters containing silica have filtered. These coat into beautiful crystal linings, often of vivid colours (figs 25, 31).

NODULES

When a geode is completely filled inside, and the rock is solid, it is known as a nodule. These are often sliced in half and polished, revealing strangely-fascinating patterns (fig. 33).

THUNDER EGGS

This form of nodule invariably has a solid agate centre and, like other nodules, in outward appearance is a pitted, earthy-looking ball of rock (fig. 27). The thunder eggs of Oregon are the nodules most prized by collectors, and are to be found in sections known as 'beds'. Sometimes within a few square yards literally thousands may be found. Although these locations are privately owned, collectors are allowed inside on the payment of a small fee. In the United States sites are usually advertized in the various lapidary magazines.

How to work most quartz varieties

In the crystalline form quartz is often brittle. There is no cleavage, but

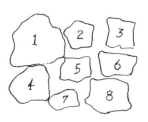

Fig 28   Cut sections of gemstones:
1 agatized wood
2 Madagascar agate
3 fluorite
4 Oregon thunder egg (halved)
5 brecciated jasper
6 rhodochrosite
7 Oregon agate
8 banded carnelian agate

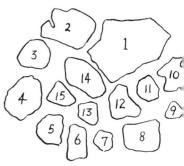

Fig 29   Group of rough minerals:
1 fluorite
2 amazonite
3 malachite
4 mica in quartz
5 peacock pyrites
6 tourmaline
7 amber
8 amber
9 carnelian
10 calcite
11 smoky quartz
12 turquoise
13 pyrites
14 fluorite
15 chalcedony rose

Fig 30   Tumbled load of beach pebbles

certain variations in the hardness of the crystals, dependent on direction. The crypto-crystalline varieties are tougher by nature, and thus easier to deal with; though they may take longer to polish. Also they are rather more porous, and care must be taken to avoid their coming in contact with oil or colouring matter, which might discolour them.

Cabochons are the ideal form of presenting most types of chalcedony. Cabochons are also well-suited to the crystalline varieties, but these can be, in addition, cut and polished in other forms. Tin oxide or cerium oxide (Linde A US) are ordinarily used as polishing agents, working on a buff of felt, wood or leather. Otherwise the procedure is similar to that described in the cabochon chapter (p. 67).

Tumbling mixes of rough agate are a good bet for beginners.

4 Descriptions of gemstones and decorative stones

This section consists of short descriptive details of gemstone material suitable for the amateur lapidary to work on. It may be remarked that many of the well-known precious and semi-precious gemstones have been omitted. This is because all these require skilled lapidary work such as faceting, and this lies outside the scope of the book.

A gemstone depends for its beauty as much on its depth of colour as on the manner in which it is cut and polished. Three main groups of these minerals emerge: the transparent, the translucent and the opaque. Pure transparent tints of the precious stones can be seen at their best in the fire of the ruby, the gold of the topaz and the brilliant green of the emerald, and also in many of the finer specimens of quartz. In the translucent group the optical effect may come from reflection rather than from intrinsic coloration, as seen in the opal – a myriad of scintillating spangles – or the moonstone – which brings forth light from the interior without producing much colour.

In the final group – the opaque stones – turquoise and jade are among the most familiar. Many in this group are porous in composition, and are often artificially dyed.

Many of the stones listed will be available only from lapidary suppliers, unless you live in an area rich in mineral deposits; but some knowledge of their properties will be useful if you intend working them. When buying from suppliers, remember that while you can buy rough minerals for tumbling by mail order, you must select personally any specimen that you want to cut and polish into a cabochon. Only the best quality stones can be used for this. Never buy these through mail order.

The equipment needed for collecting should be kept to a minimum, but the following are basic requirements: a geologist's hammer, for breaking away pieces of rock; a cold chisel for splitting them; a good magnifying glass; a pair of old gloves; an eyeshield; a knife; newspaper for wrapping specimens; plastic bags; maps and a *light* rucksack (stones are heavy!).

Choose your specimens carefully, taking two examples of the same mineral wherever possible (but not more), as they may be interesting to compare. If convenient at the time, label each specimen with particulars as to locality and date for later identification. You might want to check up with specimens in a museum. If a specimen is too large, split it with a chisel and hammer, wearing gloves and an eyeshield for this operation.

Always find out beforehand whether the collecting area is on private property. If it is, permission to search must be obtained first.

Amber

Amber differs from the minerals which will be described, being of organic origin. It is a fossilized resin, deriving from coniferous trees of the early ages. Small insects are sometimes found entombed in it, and specimens such as these are regarded as superior to ordinary amber. The colour varies from yellow to a deep reddish brown, transparent to translucent. It is found in irregular rounded masses on beaches and stretches of the Atlantic coast of the US, on the coast of England (coming down from the Baltic), while some of the finest material comes from Sicily, Rumania and Burma.

Hardness $2\frac{1}{2}$ to 3. *Lustre* resinous. It is not brittle, and has the property of becoming electrified when rubbed. It is very light in weight. Both these points make identification easy.

WORKING

Amber is good to carve. Ordinary steel blades will cut it easily, and finishing can be done with successively finer grades of sandpaper. Polish with flannel, felt and tin oxide.

Aventurine   (see quartz).
Amethyst   (see quartz).
Amazonite   (see feldspar).
Aquamarine   (see beryl).

Azurite

This is of an intense blue, and occurs with malachite in rocks containing copper sulphide. Normally it is found in massive form with a smooth mammilated surface.

Crystal system monoclinic. *Hardness* $3\frac{1}{2}$ to 4. *Cleavage* none. *Fracture* surface irregular, but quite tough, owing to fibrous composition. *Lustre* vitreous.

WORKING

It may be sawn into slabs to display the spheroid banding. Takes a good polish, but its low hardness is against its use as a gemstone. Satisfactory for cabochons, carving or tumbling. Grinding very rapid, using fine wheels and sanders only, finally polishing by hand using clean moist leather. Rough obtainable from suppliers, but not cheap.

Beryl (aquamarine)

This occurs in igneous rocks as an accessory mineral, and is sometimes found in metamorphic rocks. Although a common mineral, gem quality material is hard to find. Several varieties exist, of which each has a distinctive colour and characteristic – emerald, the gemstone, a brilliant blue-green; morganite, pink beryl; heliodor, golden beryl; aquamarine, pale green to pale blue; green beryl, yellow-green; and colourless variety called goshenite.

It is often difficult to distinguish beryl from quartz. Ordinary beryl is opaque, green, blue, yellow or white, only the transparency of the gemstone quality giving it such brilliance.

Crystal system hexagonal. *Crystal habit* well-formed six-sided crystals are common. *Hardness* 7½ to 8, with a degree of toughness which enables it to be worked without cleaving or splitting. *Cleavage* poor. *Fracture* irregular to conchoidal. *Lustre* vitreous.

WORKING

All beryls are both tough and heat-resistant, so polishing is easy. Slightly flawed ones may be cut and polished into cabochons. Their main use, however, is as fine gemstones in jewelry. Poorer material may be tumbled, and rough can be bought from suppliers at medium cost.

Calcite

A common mineral found in igneous, metamorphic and sedimentary rocks. A crystalline form of calcium carbonate, in this shape it takes huge crystals, sometimes several feet across, of dramatic beauty and clarity. Usually colourless, but sometimes assuming a colour due to impurities, yellow and brown being the commonest. 'Iceland spar', a very pure, transparent variety has the property of double refraction.

Crystal system hexagonal. *Crystal habit* variety of shapes – needle-like crystals, short-stunted crystals and twin crystals; also massive form. *Hardness* 3. *Cleavage* three evenly-spaced cleavages, which always break along the cleavage plane, make calcite a rather fragile mineral; easier to handle in massive form. *Lustre* vitreous, sugary in the massive form.

WORKING

Massive material grinds quickly and well. Can be cut and shaped, but is too soft for tumbling. Polishing must be done very gently on wax or wood. A mineral for collections rather than for lapidary work. Argentinian and Peruvian rough is cheap, also English.

Chrysoberyl

A rather uncommon mineral, occasionally found in beryl-bearing pegmatites. A gemstone mainly for professionals. Usually transparent, but often flawed. Occurring in several varieties: alexandrite appears green in daylight and red in artificial light; cat's eye is the green opalescent variety and rather rare; other colours are lemon yellow and brown.

Crystal system orthorhombic. *Crystal habit* mostly well-shaped crystals, some finely fibrous. *Hardness* 8½. *Cleavage* distinct. *Lustre* vitreous.

WORKING
Rough may be ground on ordinary wheels. Cat's eyes make ideal cabochons, and should be sanded with two grades of grit, with a third sanding on a wooden lap with diamond dust. Great heat is generated, and dopped stones must be checked against wax becoming loose. Tumbling should be done with other material of similar hardness. Generally obtainable from suppliers.

Chrysolite (olivine, peridot)

Olivine is found in many igneous rock types. It weathers rapidly and decomposes to serpentine under some conditions. Peridot, the gem variety and the birthstone for August, is fairly common; but is seldom found in pieces large enough to cut. Material from Brazil and Ceylon is usually of the green tourmaline variety. Colours are green to dark green – its finest coloration being a bright yellow-green. Mostly transparent, but often filled with small inclusions.

Crystal system orthorhombic. *Crystal habit* usually granular, occasionally crystals. *Hardness* 6½. *Cleavage* poor, though fairly tough – cleavable. *Lustre* vitreous.

WORKING
Olivine: sawing, cutting, grinding as normally, polishing should be done with care, watching the surface for pitting. If this occurs, change direction.

Peridot: usually too small to cut. Loose pebbles are often found. Both varieties in rough from suppliers.

Epidote

Most often found in metamorphosed limestone, sometimes together with garnet, also occasionally in pegmatites. Colours are brownish green to yellowish green.

Crystal system monoclinic. *Crystal habit* usually massive, although crystals sometimes occur. *Hardness* 7. *Cleavage* perfect. *Lustre* vitreous.

WORKING
Rough is trouble-free, although changes of polishing direction may be necessary. As stones are usually dark in colour, they must be cut thinly for this to show. Obtainable from suppliers. Massive (US) for tumbling and cabochons in medium-price range.

Feldspar (moonstone, amazonite, labradorite)

Feldspar, an important rock-forming mineral, is one of the main constituents of most igneous rocks, many of the metamorphic rocks and certain sedimentary ones. It is abundant in most parts of the world. Of the gem varieties, moonstone, amazonite, and labradorite are the best known.

In the mineral species, feldspar, combining with other minerals such as quartz and mica (forming granite), produces many of the most impressive rocks and pebbles. (Some of these are described under the headings of the different rocks.)

Moonstone is translucent and of a silvery bluish sheen. The shimmering play of white light is distinguishable from glass by its double refraction. Comes mainly from Ceylon, where it occurs as pebbles in gem gravels; or as rough fragments in clay, probably coming from decomposed igneous rock. Is usually cut in cabochons to reveal its fine chatoyancy.

Amazonite is a richly-coloured dark green or bluish green mineral in its finest form, and is quite translucent. Pale varieties are more common. Good quality rough is expensive.

Labradorite is probably the most beautiful variety of feldspar. Is normally a dull grey in colour but, when suitably cut and polished, the change is remarkable. The lustre becomes metallic and a fine coloured sheen appears over the surface, the colours varying from blue, green and yellow, and sometimes shades of red. It is usually cut with a flat surface or in cabochons, though a good deal of material is badly shattered. The finest quality comes from Labrador – hence the name.

Crystal system usually massive or granular, but well-formed crystals may occur in pegmatites. *Hardness* 6. *Cleavage* perfect in two directions almost at right-angles to each other. *Fracture* uneven. *Lustre* vitreous to pearly.

WORKING

All varieties polish easily and fairly smoothly, though shattering sometimes causes difficulties with cabochon cutting. Some varieties show cleavage, which can be troublesome. Use cerium oxide on felt for polishing. Rough available from suppliers.

Fluorite

An impressive mineral, occuring chiefly in pegmatites and vein-type deposits. Varied translucent colours, from white, green-yellow to the rich purplish blue of the famous Derbyshire 'blue john', a massive variety in which the colours grade from the margin to the centre. Rough is expensive in this variety.

Many specimens show fluorescence, glowing violet when exposed to ultra-violet light. This is due to the presence of rare earth minerals and manganese. The crystal form sometimes contains inclusions of other minerals.

Crystal system cubic (isometric). *Crystal habit* cubic crystals, and also in massive form. *Hardness* 4, but brittle. *Cleavage* perfect octahedral. *Lustre* vitreous.

Massive forms are granular and translucent. Single refraction.

WORKING

Owing to the very brittle nature, all stages of cutting must be done carefully, avoiding cleavage planes. Rough, which may be pre-formed and tumbled, is easily obtained from suppliers.

Garnet

Garnet is a very common metamorphic mineral, more often found in spherical red crystals through schist or gneiss, although sometimes found in pegmatites. The finest specimens are dark red and sometimes known as 'Cape ruby', but normally they are reddish or purplish brown. Fine quality material is faceted. A variety known as andradite is bright green but uncommon. Another gem-quality garnet, grossular (grossularite US), found in South Africa and called Transvaal jade, is in massive form and of a deep emerald green.

Crystal system cubic (isometric). *Crystal habit* massive – sometimes well-formed crystals. *Hardness* $7\frac{1}{2}$. *Cleavage* none. *Fracture* conchoidal. *Lustre* vitreous.

WORKING

Garnet is quite brittle except in grossular (grossularite US), the massive form, which is very tough and polishes well, making fine cabochons. These require care in grinding and sanding, which should not be done dry. There are no directional difficulties in cutting and polishing. Rough may be tumbled, and is obtainable from suppliers, but water-worn fragments often found by collectors make the best tumbling material, and are best tumbled alone. Rather expensive to buy.

Jade (jadeite, nephrite)

Jade is the general term for two distinct minerals, jadeite and nephrite, both fibrous, tough textured, and greenish in colour, but varying from white to black. Nephrite (greenstone) is the commoner, while jadeite, far more rare, was prized by the Chinese as the finest of all gemstones. The fibres of nephrite give it such strength that it is hard to break with a hammer. Typically it is milky-white to dark green, with a uniform coloration. Jadeite tends to be more emerald green.

Crystal system monoclinic. *Crystal habit* always massive, from very fine granular to coarse granular. *Hardness* nephrite $5\frac{1}{2}$ to $6\frac{1}{2}$, jadeite 6 to $6\frac{1}{2}$. *Cleavage* perfect. *Lustre* nephrite, oily translucent to opaque; jadeite, vitreous, translucent to opaque.

Nephrite: exceedingly tough, it owes its strength to its fine-grained nature. It can be ground fairly easily, but sanding and polishing may be more difficult. Experiment with wet and dry sanding, as different material will vary. Fine for carving. The best specimens come from East Turkestan, and New Zealand is also a common source. US grey-green massive variety is medium-priced.

Jadeite: being less tough than nephrite, fine sanding must be done with plenty of water to give it a fine smooth surface. Very impressive when slabbed and polished. Rough may be tumbled, and both varieties may be bought from suppliers.

Jet

A black organic composition, resulting from the decomposition of drift-wood, which, sinking to the sea bed, became integrated in the rock into which the fine mud was transformed. Occurs in hard shales known as 'jet rock'. The best material comes from the upper lias on the coast near Whitby in England, but other occurrences are found in south east Colorado and Santa Fe, New Mexico, US. Best quality is uniformly black and polishes well.

Hardness 3 to 4. *Lustre* silky.

WORKING

It is reasonably tough, but soft and easily scratched. May be cut with ordinary steel blades, as with amber, and polished with tin oxide on a cloth. Very suitable for carving.

Lapis lazuli

An opaque gemstone of intense ultramarine blue, sometimes showing a sprinkling of brassy yellow specks (pyrites). Artificial staining is often done to improve poor-coloured material. As it is actually composed of three different minerals, it is technically a rock.

Crystal system cubic (isometric). *Crystal habit* usually massive. *Hardness* 6. *Cleavage* poor. *Lustre* greasy to vitreous.

WORKING

As lapis lazuli is massive in structure, it has no tendency to split and part. Cabochons are the ideal form in which to present it, but great care is needed in grinding, as the material wears away very quickly owing to its soft nature. Sanding must be done very thoroughly when you have to wear down inclusions of pyrites, which will have a greater degree of hardness. Use tin oxide on leather for polishing. Rough is obtainable, but is expensive and usually sold by the carat.

Malachite

Like azurite, malachite is a similarly impressive mineral, showing a brilliant opaque green in place of the blue, both colours being due to the dissolution of copper ores. Working down through the surface, these solutions have deposited layer on layer of spherical masses which, when sliced through, give the characteristic concentric bands of malachite.

Crystal system monoclinic, but crystals are small and uncommon. *Crystal habit* usually massive with streaky texture. *Hardness* $3\frac{1}{2}$ to 4. *Cleavage* little or none. *Lustre* silky to vitreous.

WORKING

Material must be thick to cut, and only the banded masses are of any interest. As it is weak and brittle in thin sections, fairly thick cabochons should be cut, and are quite easy to work. Owing to its softness, it tends to grind away very quickly and may produce misshapen stones unless you are very careful. Rough may be bought, but tumbling can only be done with stones of similar hardness. Very expensive. Katangan is the cheapest variety.

Obsidian

This is a natural glass, the result of volcanic lava cooling too rapidly to allow crystallization. Had it cooled more slowly, the product would have been a rock composed of quartz, feldspar and mica, as in granite. It is coloured dark green to black; but grey, yellow, brown and red are occasionally found. Is fairly transparent, but often has small inclusions like bubbles which reflect the light. It is often uneven and striated in texture. An interesting form is 'Apache Tears', small nodules of translucent, brownish material smaller than a walnut in size.

Crystal system and habit massive, except the 'Apache Tears'. *Hardness* 5, very brittle. *Fracture* well developed conchoidal. *Lustre* naturally vitreous.

WORKING

Obsidian cuts fairly easily, but great care must be taken in sanding and polishing. Wet sanding is essential, or it will crack with the heat generated. Polishing should be done with tin oxide. It is fairly widespread in most countries, but rough is easily obtainable from suppliers, and may be tumbled. It must be tumbled alone, and the speed of drum reduced to polishing speed at all grit stages. Polish with tin oxide in the ratio of 1 pound of oxide and $\frac{1}{2}$ pound sugar (as a thickener) to 5 pounds stones. Makes good cabochons.

Opal

Many varieties of this beautiful gemstone exist. White opal, fire opal, water opal, Mexican opal are just a few. When pure it is nearly colourless, and always tends to be milky and opaque, the coloured varieties resulting from mineral impurities. Opal differs from other gemstones in that it is not a crystal but a kind of solidified jelly, which, after cooling, changed its texture and formed into a series of very thin films. Each one of these differed slightly in their refraction of light. The actual tint of opal depends on the thickness of the film, and the diversity of a myriad of tiny cracks which produce the spangling and opalescence of the gemstone.

Crystal system none, as it is amorphous. *Crystal habit* botryoidal or massive. *Hardness* $5\frac{1}{2}$ to 6. *Cleavage* none. *Lustre* vitreous.

Single refraction.

WORKING
Opal is usually cabochon-cut, either in flat or steep form, dictated by the extent of the colour. Great skill in cutting is essential to get the best direction of the colour with minimum of material. Very susceptible to overheating, and easily damaged by this. Some varieties tend to absorb water, and may be discoloured if dipped into dirty water or if ink or coloured fluids drip on them. Use No. 600 grit for the fine grind and less of it than usual, and omit the rough grind entirely. Opal may be tumbled with other soft stones, and a shorter time for grinding may be expected. Good quality opal is expensive, and great care must be taken in buying raw material. Cheap opal in debris form is obtainable for tumbling. Mexican opal is sometimes cheaper in this form.

Pearl

Pearl is not a gemstone in the strictest sense of the word, but has been accepted as a gem of the highest rank in jewelry from historic times. It is popular today. Native pearls are, of course, formed organically inside the oyster by a natural process. Cultured pearls are also formed inside the oyster, but by synthetic means, such as forcing the jaws of the shells apart and inserting a foreign object which will eventually become coated with layers of nacre (mother-of-pearl). Imitation pearls are manufactured in several ways, a common one being to coat glass beads with various pearly substances. Imitations are easily detected by inspecting the drilled hole, the edges of which will show signs of flaking away, revealing the glass within.

Pearls are opaque and soft, having a Hardness of 4, but possessing the unique lustre that makes them so treasured. No working on them is necessary.

Pyrites

An opaque mineral of brass yellow or bronze yellow in colour, often found in very perfect crystals. Commonly known as 'fool's gold', as it has been mistaken for gold. Certain fossils – ammonites especially –

coated with gold pyrites, make arresting specimens. It has also been wrongly confused with marcasite. Very widespread in nature, it is found in igneous and sedimentary rocks of many types, and also in quartz veins and pegmatites.

Crystal system cubic (isometric), but does not have its complete symmetry. *Crystal habit* both massive and granular, and also in well-formed striated crystal faces. *Hardness* 6½. *Cleavage* very poor. *Lustre* metallic.

WORKING

Pyrites crystals may be set in jewelry, as in Victorian times, but are not commonly used today. Rocks or fossils with sparkling pyrites inclusions or coatings should be included in a collection of specimens. The massive variety is cheap.

Rhodochrosite

The lovely rose red of this stone is comparable to rhodonite, although the colour is more delicate and the sheen finer. It is characterized by a circular banded pattern, each sphere being of a different and more subtle shade of pink. These botryoidal forms are not unlike malachite, the formation suggesting that the masses are composed of stalagmites which came about by the manganese carbonate crystallizing from mineral-rich water.

Crystal system hexagonal, in the rhombohedral division. *Crystal habit* crystalline and massive. *Hardness* 4. *Cleavage* three directions of easy cleavage, like calcite. *Lustre* pearly on the cleavage surfaces but otherwise vitreous.

Transparent to translucent. Double refraction. Usually found in veins, or as crystalline crusts.

WORKING

Unfortunately this material is both soft and fragile, and requires care in handling. As it is also brittle, grinding for cabochons and polishing of faced slabs must be done only on fine wheels. The different banding may show varying degrees of hardness, according to the amount of iron they contain when sanded. Rhodochrosite does take a fine polish, however, and this should be carried out on a leather buff using tin oxide. A finely-patterned polished specimen may be seen in the colour plate of polished sections (fig. 28).

Rhodonite

A handsome ornamental stone when cut and polished. Normally found in shades of rose pink, flesh red and brown-red, with a tracery of black veining, due to manganese.

Crystal system triclinic. *Crystal habit* fine-grained massive and coarse granular. *Hardness* $5\frac{1}{2}$ to $6\frac{1}{2}$. *Cleavage* one perfect. *Lustre* vitreous to pearly on the cleavage surfaces.

WORKING

May be slabbed and polished. The massive forms are tough, but the granular ones very weak, and both have undercutting tendencies. The deeper-coloured material often polishes better. Cabochon cutting is commonly used for this material, which requires long sanding on a No. 400 wet sanding cloth, with plenty of water. Leather should be used for polishing. May be tumbled, and in the polishing stage use one part tin oxide to one part detergent. Requires long tumbling. Varied rough may be bought from suppliers in medium price range.

Serpentine

This is a massive rock formed as a result of the metamorphism of other rocks, such as olivine. As it occurs in enormous masses, is very soft, and of attractive veined patterning, it is widely used as a building stone for facades. The many varieties are known by different names: verde antique is green, mottled with white veining of calcite; bowenite (Hardness $5\frac{1}{2}$ to 6), like williamsite, is bright green and translucent; and Korea jade is very similar to nephrite. Other varieties are commonly red or flecked with red. Precious serpentine is the term used to describe the lighter varieties, which are more compact and translucent, lending themselves ideally to cutting and polishing.

Crystal system monoclinic in symmetry. *Crystal habit* massive and dense, finely granular. *Hardness* $2\frac{1}{2}$ to 4. *Lustre* vitreous.

WORKING

Serpentine is soft and very easy to carve or saw. Water alone is the best coolant for sawing, as the stone is porous and apt to absorb oil, which will be difficult to remove. Grinding must be done carefully when impurities are present, as the hardness will be variable, although the material is quite tough. Serpentine may be tumbled with other soft stones. First grind with a No. 600 grit ($\frac{1}{4}$ pound to 5 pounds stones), then polish with $\frac{1}{4}$ pound tin oxide to one cup of dry detergent. This will take from 150 to 200 hours. Available from suppliers cheaply, but it is very abundant in many areas.

Spodumene

The two gem varieties are hiddentite, a bluish green, rather rare, and kunzite-lilac, violet and pink. Often in pegmatites in older granite areas.

Crystal system monoclinic. *Crystal habit* often in elongated crystals, also massive form. *Hardness* $6\frac{1}{2}$ to 7. *Cleavage* perfect, parallel to prism faces. *Lustre* vitreous. Marked dichroism.

Fig 31

Fig 32

Fig 33

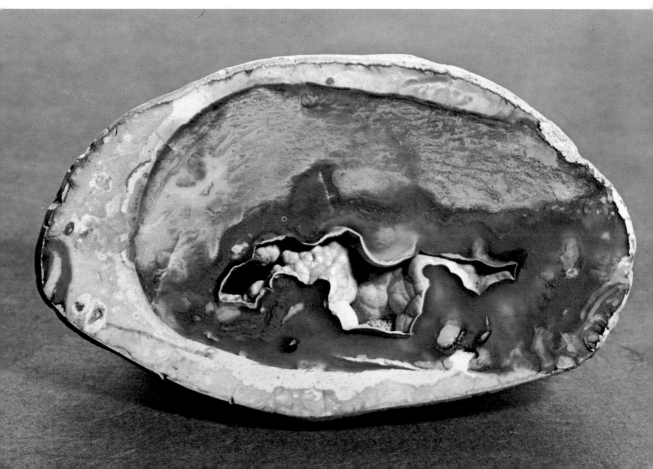

Cabochons are the usual form in which spodumene is presented, and the rough supplied for this is normally in coarse, silky masses. This fibrous material is ground and polished in the usual way. Sawing crystals is more difficult, and the feed-in should be done slowly. It may also be tumbled. Obtainable from suppliers, but very expensive.

Topaz

A very popular yellow stone, found chiefly in pegmatites, frequently confused with citrine. Occuring in other shades, such as pale brown, blue and pink (this tint usually produced by heating) and a colourless variety often flawed with small cracks.

Crystal system orthorhombic. *Crystal habit* massive, granular or well-developed prismatic crystals. *Hardness* 8. *Cleavage* one perfect. *Lustre* vitreous.

WORKING
Grinds easily and fast, although it polishes slowly. Fairly tough. Beware of generated heat melting dopping wax and the stone being displaced. Although mainly used for faceting, cabochons are also made. Material may be obtained from suppliers and is rather expensive. Usually sold by carat.

Tourmaline

A semi-precious stone, displaying such a galaxy of colour that it is probably unsurpassed by any other gem. This great variety of colour is due to differences in composition, but the delicate 'water-melon' tints are the best known. Other shades are reddish, green, blue, brown, yellow, black and colourless. Sometimes with coloured bands of crystal. It is found in pegmatites in granite, invariably in crystalline form.

Crystal system trigonal. *Crystal habit* elongated striated crystals most common. *Hardness* 7½. *Cleavage* none. *Lustre* vitreous to resinous.

Strong dichroism. Crystals often show different colours at each end.

WORKING
Tourmaline is transparent, and often flawed and brittle. These factors must be considered when cutting and polishing. As the colour changes considerably in its direction, preforms must be orientated accordingly. Grinds and polishes well if over-heating is avoided. Some material which is distinctly fibrous in structure makes good cabochons. Flawed rough may be tumbled. Tumbling quality is medium-priced from suppliers, but gemstone varieties very expensive.

Turquoise

This mineral of a pure opaque blue or green is usually found in zones of weathered rocks containing copper minerals, mainly in the more arid areas of the world. It has a tendency to absorb liquids or grease and changes colour accordingly. The composition is a concretionary mass of tiny crystals and is therefore crypto-crystalline.

Crystal system triclinic. *Crystal habit* massive with incrustations. *Hardness* $5\frac{1}{2}$ to 6. *Cleavage* not noticeable. *Lustre* waxy.

Colour, which tends to fade, is often restored by artificial means, but the result is not permanent.

WORKING

As it is an opaque stone, it is always cabochon-cut. It takes a good polish, which is durable to a certain extent, as scratches show little on the stone because of its comparative opacity. Not brittle, and polishes well on leather with chrome oxide. May also be carved and engraved. Very expensive. Birthstone for December.

5 Lapidary equipment and its uses

Not all collectors wish to shape and polish the specimens they find. For some the basic beauty of the stones is sufficient, and they wish to leave them in their natural state – possibly with a little cleaning.

But the majority will wish to bring out the dormant qualities of the material by enhancing it in some way, either simply for pleasure or in the hope that the hobby may become a profitable one.

Some basic equipment is essential, and some sort of workshop must be organized if you are to use your equipment to the best possible advantage. Unless you simply want to run a tumbler, of course. Even if you intend to start only tentatively, with a minimum of machinery, adding more efficient and expensive equipment as your skill and enthusiasm increase, certain planning must be done beforehand.

The size and complexity of the machinery, and where it should be placed in relation to the floor space, must be considered, and also the use of wall space. Provision must be made for good lighting, and adequate power points from which to run the machines. Swivelling spotlights of 150-watt capacity which can be directed onto the work in progress are an asset, and must be strategically placed. Lamps of the goose-neck type, set on the work-bench, should be used for focussing on work of a closer nature.

Water and drainage are necessary, preferably laid on, although it *is* possible to work without them, by various arrangements of drip tanks and sponges, with troughs and buckets for surplus water.

The set-up and arrangement of the equipment is of great importance. As the polishing unit must be kept absolutely clean, and free from dust and dirt and grit particles, the more messy operations of sawing, grinding and sanding should ideally be carried out in another part of the workshop. If this is not possible (you may have a combination unit with the polisher on the same arbor, or shaft), all polishing equipment should be kept under protective covering when not in use.

The abrasive grit used in lapidary work is a silicon carbide grit, sometimes known as carborundum grit, or by other trade names. It is sized by being screened through different gauge meshes. The size numbers most commonly used in the various operations are as follows:

Fig 35 Slab saw. Robilt model

No. 80–100 grit – coarse, for tumbling
   and lapping (see pp. 57, 58)
No. 120–200 grit – coarse for grinding
No. 300 grit – fine grinding
No. 400 – first sanding
No. 600–800 – fine sanding.

This grit is used in powder form for tumbling, but is incorporated in the different wheels used for grinding and sanding. Thus in ordering wheels you must specify a No. 220 grit or a No. 400 grit and so on, according to your requirements. At the same time you must also state the thickness of the wheel, the diameter, and the arbor hole (the arbor is the shaft).

A few further points should be considered when setting up a workshop. Check that the electric power is not overloaded by the various motors you may be running, and that adequate safety precautions regarding insulation have been taken.

Build in as much storage space as can be arranged – shelves where the rock specimens can be displayed, shelves for the grits near the machines using them, sturdy work-benches for machines and for hand work. An old-fashioned stoneware sink makes a pleasing receptacle for holding rocks and stones for tumbling. Finally, keep to the simplest equipment when you begin. The combination units are economical as regards space, but are not a vast improvement on single machines with interchangeable wheels.

Tumblers

Many types of these are available (p. 60) and some are described in detail in chapter 6. Drums or barrels of several shapes are available – the heavy-duty polythene ones suitable for smaller tumblers are usually cylindrical. Hexagonal drums are commonly made of steel with rubber linings, which frequently can be removed. These are far superior to the polythene ones and are much longer-lasting.

Tumble-polishing may be carried out indoors in any room available, provided there is no objection to the inevitable noise which accompanies it. This may be minimized to a certain extent by setting the machine on a thick rubber base, but a large tumbler will make its presence felt, and is better used in an outhouse or cellar. So if you have a workshop or garage available with space for the tumbler, this is the best place for it. A supply of running water will facilitate washing the stones when changing grits. Tumbling is dealt with in chapter 6 (p. 58).

The slab saw

A slabbing saw is a very expensive bit of equipment, and unless you want to saw large quantities, or contemplate taking up lapidary work professionally, it would be better to join a club doing practical lapidary and use their saw. A good trim saw is quite adequate for most smaller scale work, and is the type described in the technical section Cutting a Cabochon (p. 67).

The slabbing saw illustrated (fig. 35) has a cast aluminium vice to hold the rock, which slides along past the saw on a rigid rail, producing perfectly straight cuts every time. It has a 10-in. diamond blade, capable of slabbing sections up to $4 \times 3\frac{1}{2} \times 8$ ins. The lid is fitted with a viewing window, and has a hinged saw splash-guard. It can be converted for trimming smaller pieces by fitting the trim saw table provided. The overall size is 15 ins long × 20 ins wide and is 15 ins in height.

Trim saw

Various types of these are available – the one you choose depends on the jobs you require of it, and the price you are able to pay. The ones illustrated (figs 36, 37) are in all respects similar to the one used in chapter 7. It takes an 8-in. or a 10-in. diamond blade, which enables it to slice a slab or trim a cabochon.

The coolant used should be that recommended by the manufacturers,

and sufficient of this solution should be maintained to keep the blade rim covered to a depth of about an inch – enough coolant, in fact, so that when the blade is in operation a fine spray falls onto the stone. Too much coolant will splash onto the operator. This saw requires a quarter horse-power motor, which must be purchased separately.

Fig 36 Trim saw. Robilt Model. Courtesy Cambridge Lapidary Club

Diamond blades

Care of your blades is important. They are built to run true at the correct operating speed, but a number of things can cause them to lose their tension and start vibrating. The rock slipping, moving cross-feed when

Fig 37 Trim saw. Courtesy Ammonite Ltd.

the blade is in the rock, the carrier riding up, inadequate coolant, damage to blade in mounting, and mis-alignment of carrier with plan of rotation of blade – all these can cause damage.

Before installing a new blade, the shaft of the machine should be checked for any looseness that may indicate worn bearings or shaft. To ensure even wear of the cutting edge, reverse the blade occasionally by removing and replacing so that it cuts in the opposite direction. This will prolong the life of the blade.

Blades must never be run without a coolant, and this must be kept clean, the sludge being periodically removed and replaced with fresh coolant. Finally, always try to keep a spare blade to hand, so that you are not tempted to run on a damaged one and ruin it entirely.

Combination units

Grinding involves the shaping of the stone to the desired configuration, usually on a wheel of No. 80–100 grit, and a second finer grinding is done to shape it further on a wheel of No. 200 grit. Use water as a coolant for both these operations. The maximum use of these wheels can be obtained

Fig 38 Combination unit without saw. Courtesy Cambridge Lapidary Club

by working the stones evenly over the entire surface, and you should develop sufficient skill to avoid grooves and gouges.

Sanding is done to remove the scratches after grinding, and to smooth the stone preparatory to polishing. Usually a No. 400-grit wheel is used for coarse sanding, and a No. 600-grit for finishing. It may be done on a disc, a drum or a belt-sander, running at 2400 rpm to 4000 rpm. As great heat is generated in dry sanding, the stones may crack, so care must be exercised and occasional inspections made to avoid overheating. Wet sanding is always preferable.

Polishing is the final and most rewarding stage in gem-working, and should take only a few minutes if the stone has been properly prepared in the previous operations. On a felt buff (usually used for flat stones) the speed should be 750 to 1000 rpm; on a leather buff (usually used for dopped stones) 1000 to 2000 rpm, using as polishing agent tin oxide or cerium oxide, mixed with water to a thick cream and applied to the buff with a brush.

The three operations (grinding, sanding and polishing) are usually accomplished on a machine combining the different wheels on the same arbor; and frequently a trim saw is also incorporated. Some prefer to do the polishing on a separate wheel which can be kept scrupulously clean. A small particle of grit from the other operations can ruin the polish completely.

Fig 39 Combination unit, Highland Park Model with saw. Courtesy Ammonite Ltd.

56

Lapping

Lapping is a very simple process, and consists of rubbing the stone against a revolving flat plate charged with loose abrasive. This is applied with water, in the form of a slurry, to the centre of the spinning lap and spread outwards with a brush. The lap itself is a horizontal revolving disc, supported on a steel shaft over a splash pan. This pan is often removable, so that it can be periodically cleaned out. The main purpose of lapping is to grind and polish specimens which have been sawn so that they present a fairly flat surface – for instance slabs of agate, patterned transparencies, or book-end sections.

It is essentially the same procedure as grinding and tumbling, except that it is considerably faster. Using a loose No. 200 grit and water on the laps, the slabs are often completed within a few hours – the time for this initial grinding depending on the smoothness and hardness of the original material.

After a second grinding in No. 600 grit, the slabs may be polished in a cloth-covered pan with tin oxide or other polishing agent.

The specimen should be dipped in water from time to time, and the face wiped clear to observe progress and clean away the grit. Also be sure to stop the motor and wash the plate clean between the different grits. Avoid wear of the plate in one place by using the whole area of the lap at the same time.

The newer vibratory laps, completely automatic, come from America and make the process considerably faster. The technique is the same, but the machines are much more expensive.

6 Tumble polishing

The process of polishing stones in a rotary-action tumbler closely follows the method of nature. The abrasive action of the oceans and rivers, by continuous movement, brings about a uniformity of form and smoothness in pebbles and rocks. The mechanical rotation of the tumbler reproduces this action in miniature, accomplishing within a few weeks a patina that would take nature countless ages to achieve.

Little skill is required to operate a tumbler; a minimum need be spent on equipment; and provided that materials are carefully selected, fine polished stones should result. Most varieties can be tumbled; even those considered unsuitable for polishing by other methods, and which might be discarded, can be used. Stones and gemstones which have been tumble-polished are irregular in shape and are called 'baroques', except for the

Fig 42 Tumbled stones with holes

Fig 43 Tumbled stones

smoothly rounded beach pebbles. 'Preforms' are stones cut to size and shaped on a trim saw before being tumble-polished – these are always obtainable from suppliers. As they tend to be rather flat, a full tumbler load of this material will not give satisfactory results – the flat edges will not grind out sufficiently. The load should also consist of a good quantity of rounded pebbles of uniform hardness.

Although it is usually safe to put mixed sizes together in the same load, they should always be of fairly uniform hardness and either all water-worn or all rough, but not a mixture of these.

As hardness is one of the most important points to be considered when choosing batches of material, you must check on the scale of hardness (Mohs' Scale is used throughout) in chapter 1, p. 19, under the description of each particular stone – always provided you can identify it.

Size is rather important too. Stones of $1\frac{1}{2}$ ins to 3 ins should be mixed with smaller stones. Larger stones, of 3 ins to 6 ins, can be tumbled successfully in big drums if stones of $1\frac{1}{2}$-in. diameter are included. If the big stones are deeply pitted, it will take considerably longer to grind them out. You may be fortunate enough to collect a quantity of large, flawless beach stones, and then the tumbling time will be reduced considerably. Some stones, softer or damaged ones, may disintegrate during the tumbling process. Keep an eye open for any of these, and remove them as soon as you see the danger of such disintegration.

Types of tumbler

It is not at all difficult to build a tumbler to suit your requirements, although some little skill and knowledge are necessary. This is the cheapest way of acquiring one, and several books on lapidary give diagrams for doing this.

Recently such a variety of tumblers have come onto the market, produced by well-known lapidary firms at reasonable prices, that it is scarcely worthwhile making one.

Fig 44   Tumbler, Model GT3.
Courtesy Gemrocks Ltd.

Fig 45 Tumbler, Model A with heavy-duty drum. Courtesy M. L. Beach Products Ltd.

Fig 46 Model B with heavy-duty drum. Courtesy M. L. Beach Products Ltd.

When buying a tumbler you must first decide exactly what your requirements are. If you have had no practical experience at all, a small, single-drum tumbler would be a cheap and easy way to gain some knowledge. These cost only a few pounds.

You may have done some tumbling already, possibly using a friend's machine, or working in a lapidary club. In this case you may wish to work with larger stones or tumble several batches at the same time, perhaps of differing varieties. A multiple tumbler, or one with larger drums, might be what you would need.

Vibratory tumblers are a fairly recent innovation in England, although they have been used in the US for some time. They work on the principle of very high speed vibrations (the average is 3000 per minute), so that the actual movement of the stones can hardly be seen. They grind considerably faster, with a minimum of noise and little chipping or fracturing, with abrasives or polishes in a semi-dry suspension. The drums, known as 'hoppers', may be left open, allowing easy inspection, and there is no splashing or build-up of gas. Preforms can be polished in forty-eight hours, losing little shape or weight.

The present disadvantage of vibratory tumblers is their expense, which is considerable, and the fact that they do need fairly constant attention during their short period of polishing.

The carborundum grits used for tumble-polishing are obtainable from lapidary suppliers (see p. 100) and some builders' merchants.

Assuming you are using a drum of one-pound capacity, the stages of tumbling are as follows:

Fig 47
Fig 48

Fig 47
Fig 48

opposite
Fig 47 Slabs and cabochons:
jasper
nephrite
rhodochrosite
turquoise

Fig 48 Cabochons of agate and carnelian

Fig 49 Vibrasonic tumbler, Model GTV1. Courtesy Gemrocks Ltd.

Fig 50 Loading the tumbler

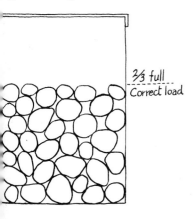

⅔ full
Correct load

STAGE 1

The material to be polished must be sorted for suitability and thoroughly washed. It is then placed in the drum, filling it approximately two-thirds to three-quarters full (fig. 50). Next, pour in just sufficient water to cover the stones, and add 1 ounce of silicon carbide grit No. 80 and 1 teaspoonful of detergent powder to each pound of stones. Attach lid firmly, taking care that no grit is lodged in the threads and that it is quite watertight, but that it is not screwed down so tightly that it may be difficult to remove. In some tumblers the lid is clamped on. Place the drum between the rollers with the lid at the *opposite* end from the motor, and switch on to start tumbling action (fig. 51). Be sure to read the manufacturer's instructions, and double-check these, especially regarding the correct revolving speed (rpm).

The time taken on this first stage will depend on the type of stones being tumbled, and may be anything from seven to ten days. Keep a notebook for tumbling, and a complete log of relevant details, such as type and hardness of load, date of commencement, amounts of grit and water (there can be variations here, depending on the type of load). Open the drum each day to inspect progress. Gases can form, which must be released.

Sometimes the drum tends to slip, and, though the rollers are revolving, the load remains stationary. Or it turns so slowly that the cascading action changes to a rocking to and fro. Binding insulating tape round the sides of the drum will generally correct these faults.

At the end of a week or so, open the drum and take out a little grit. If it has been reduced to a fine powder, the load is ready to remove. Tip it into a coarse sieve or a kitchen colander and wash thoroughly under running water, a spray or hose. Inspect carefully; the softer the stones the less satisfactory the polish obtainable, but the rough edges should have been rounded off and all surface dirt and pitting have been removed, leaving at least seventy five per cent of the stones fit for the next grinding. The rest will have to be discarded. However, if in doubt, give a day or two more.

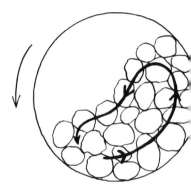

Fig 51 Cascading action of stones in tumbler

STAGE 2

Clean the drum very carefully before replacing the washed load – cleanliness cannot be over-emphasized here, as the presence of fragments of coarser grit in any stage of grinding will ruin the process. Recharge with water, adding more than for Stage 1, and a finer grit – No. 200–300, 1 ounce to one pound again and 1 teaspoonful of detergent powder. If the level of the load is now reduced, either add a few more smooth stones of equal hardness or reduce the speed to a slightly slower rpm. Most motors have adjustable pulleys for this purpose. Run for about seven days, inspecting regularly as before. When the stones are perfectly smooth, and of a frosted appearance when cleaned and dried, wash carefully and replace in drum for Stage 3.

STAGE 3

Cover with water and Grit No. 500–600 plus detergent in the usual proportion, and run for from four to six days, inspecting regularly. Some add a buffering agent at this stage, to prevent chipping, such as a handful of polystyrene chips. After washing, drying and inspecting, the stones should feel silky smooth, ready for the final stage of polishing.

STAGE 4 POLISHING

Extra attention must be given to the washing before the polishing, and ideally a separate drum should be kept for the polishing stage, as the slightest speck of grit lodged in any part of the drum or lid can ruin the whole load. Inspect every stone separately, discarding any that are flawed, still pitted, deeply scratched or chipped. Slide the load gently into the drum to avoid any damage. Add tin oxide as the polishing agent, at the rate of about one half ounce to the pound, or slightly more. Cover with sufficient water to give a creamy mix, and some filler substance, such as polystyrene chips or vermiculite (from garden suppliers). This will prevent chipping or fracturing. Run tumbler at a slightly slower rpm for three or more days, until you are satisfied that the polish will not improve. Wash the polished stones and the drum, leaving the first washing water in a bucket to settle, so that the polishing agent can be recovered and re-used (as tin oxide is expensive).

FINAL STAGE

After the final washing, replace the load carefully in a clean drum with water and about a handful of detergent powder, to make a thick, creamy solution, and run the tumbler for a further few hours to give a fine sparkle. Wash off under running water and spread stones on a clean towel to inspect the finished result. Some may be imperfect, flawed or worn, but there should be many of fine silky sheen, ideal for cabochons or for setting as baroques in jewelry.

Notes on tumbling

Hammer-broken stones such as agate, jasper, flint, produce many sections with jagged edges. These are unsatisfactory for tumbling, as the rough edges will persist right through the coarse and fine grinds.

Preforms seldom need tumbling with a coarse grit. Start on No. 400 grit, and check daily as to shaping.

Keep a good supply of hard beach pebbles in reserve to bring a tumbler load up to the correct capacity when you have not got a full load of good material.

Some tumblers are rubber-lined. If yours is not, it will be a great advantage to line it. Obtain sheet rubber of one-eighth inch thickness, or less. Cut it to shape and glue it round the inside of the drum with Bostik or Evostick adhesive. This will assist the cascading action and prevent the formation of 'flats' (i.e. like coins). Certain stones tend to slip badly in unlined drums.

Stones should be of mixed sizes and shapes within the tolerances mentioned on p. 59. The object is that the smaller ones will grind into the hollows and crevices of the larger ones.

Observe and follow instructions as to correct loading of the tumbler. If under-loaded, the stones will slide along the side of the drum to emerge as 'flats'. If overloaded, there will be insufficient room for the stones to move around and grind against each other. A cascading action is the correct tumbling movement.

If chipping or fracturing occur at any time during the process, the speed of rotation is probably too fast. Remove any damaged stones before they ruin the whole batch. Easily-fractured material must be run at lower speeds.

Check on the habit of a particular stone in chapter 2.

Glass jars and preserving jars are *not* satisfactory as tumblers – contrary to what you may have been told. They invariably have a weak spot where they will break eventually, spilling out all the grit solution and making a horrible mess. If any grit is spilled on any part of the tumbling machine, it must be cleaned off thoroughly, or it may damage the motor.

It is provident to mount a tumbling machine on a tray to catch leakages should the drum lid come off, or the drum break.

Remember that tumbling can be very noisy. If you have a basement, garage or shed, these would be the best situations in which to run your tumbler.

When breaking up material for tumbling, use a cold chisel and try and break along the line of natural cleavage or fracture. Wear gloves and an eyeshield, and do not allow anyone to stand nearby. Flying splinters can be very dangerous.

Never leave the grit solution in the drum for any length of time. It will soon set hard, and ruin the drum. Always clean it immediately after use, and store up-ended until needed.

The waste deposit from carborundum grit can block your drains, and is not particularly good for your garden. Allow it to settle, and then wrap in thick layers of newspaper and put in your rubbish bin.

Finally, do not expect to produce baroque gems from any old material – stones must be in perfect condition for these. This means free of small pits and soft spots, and of close texture. Select carefully, remembering that to have good results the material must be good to start with. If you put rubbish and flawed scraps into the tumbler, that is all you will get out of it.

7 Cutting a cabochon

Cabochon-making is one of the oldest forms of fashioning gemstones, the word originating from the Latin 'caput', a head. Although in the early days it was the only method used, it is still a very popular one today, but is more confined to the opaque and semi-precious stones. Some of the materials commonly used for cabochons are agate, jasper, rose quartz, amazonite, tiger eye, moonstone and opal.

In its simple form (described below), a cabochon has one flat and one curved surface. Double cabochons have two curved surfaces, and both types may differ in the degree of curvature, some being very domed and others shallow.

The stages of creating a cabochon are sawing a slice off the rough specimen to the required size, marking the shape on a template, cutting the outline to this shape, grinding to the desired form (usually holding the stone on a dopstick), sanding to remove all grooves and scratches, and finally polishing. Below is a detailed description of making a cabochon from a section of rough agate, which will serve as an example of the following lapidary techniques: sawing, dopping, grinding, sanding and polishing.

An agate section with an interesting design has been selected, the size of the slice to be cut measuring approximately 4×6 ins. However, the final thickness intended will be a $\frac{1}{4}$ to $\frac{1}{3}$ in., sawn in a circular domed form.

A trim saw (see figs 36, 37), probably the most useful all-purpose saw, is employed, using an 8-in. diamond blade. It is possible to cut fairly large slabs of rock with such a saw, and also small sections of cabochon size, dispensing with the need for the larger slab saw. If large rocks for bookends or similar objects are to be slabbed, then a slab saw is a necessary part of your equipment. The trim saw is described on p. 53.

SAWING

The rock to be worked must first be marked with the line the saw cut should follow. Use a coloured or an aluminium pencil to do this. Now place the rock flat on the sawing table, ensuring that the surface is clean and free from chips or fragments, which may prevent a free passage of the material through the saw. Add the coolant (as recommended by the manufacturer),

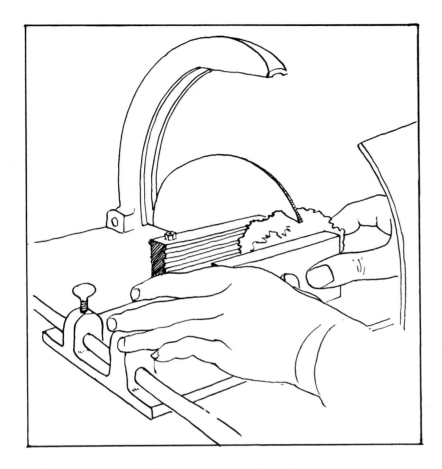

Fig 52 Sawing

switch on motor and allow the saw to run for a few moments.

Feed the rock in gently at first along the marked line, increasing the pressure to move it forward at a rather faster rate. Some saws are fitted with a carrier, as illustrated (fig. 52). Using both hands, hold it firmly: the pressure you use depends on the hardness and thickness of the specimen. For instance, an agate is fairly hard (Hardness 7), and it may be difficult at first to saw a straight line. If the cut goes in on the wrong angle, do not attempt to correct it, or your blade will be damaged along the side of the rim. Start again.

When the slab is sawn through and leaves the saw, it will probably have small projections where it has broken off at the end of the cut. These must be nibbled off with pliers, so that it may be laid flat on the table for marking.

The next step is to examine both sides of the slice through a magnifying glass to decide which is the best pattern area to use, judging both from the artistic and the practical angle. You must first search for any flaws or tiny cracks – a transparent section, such as an agate, should be held up to the light. Mark all these with the aluminium pencil, and avoid them when choosing which pattern area to cut (fig. 53).

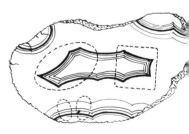

Fig 53 Drawing the pattern area

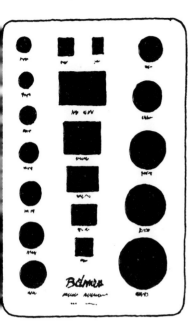

Fig 54 Template

Fig 55 Shaping bevel

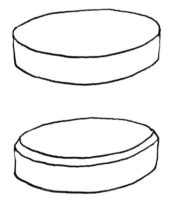

Fig 56 Grinding the outline

Templates are available in metal or plastic, cut in a variety of cabochon shapes, and you can use these for your outline form, or you can draw one yourself (fig. 54). Lay the template over the chosen area and mark round the opening with a pencil, not forgetting that the side of the slab being marked will be the bottom, so keep the pencil as close to the edge as possible.

Now return to the trim saw, and, holding the slab very firmly, cut off the larger projections by a series of flat cuts, until the rough outline emerges. Do not go too near the edge. If the outline seems untidy, hold the slice in one hand and nibble off the unwanted projections with pliers. A glove should be used for this.

OUTLINING

The crudely-shaped blank is now ready for its first grinding, which is a roughly sectional shaping, using the coarse grinding wheel – usually No. 80–100 carborundum grit – and rpm according to the manufacturers' instructions.

The machine illustrated (fig. 56) is a combination unit, and has a grinding and a sanding wheel and a polishing buff. It is covered with a splash hood, to prevent the water that must always be used from spraying. These wheels must never, on any account, be used dry.

Switch on the motor and allow to run for a few moments. Holding the stone with the outline mark uppermost and clearly visible, press it lightly against the wheel, grinding to remove any untidy edges (fig. 56).

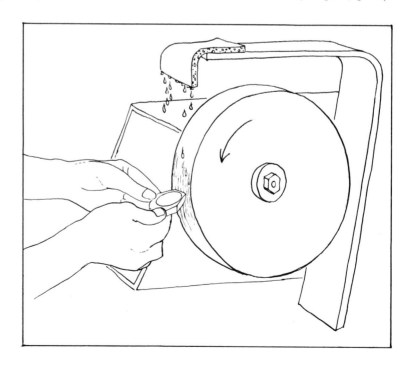

Now grind to the pencilled outline to get the basic shape, never going right up to the edge, and trying to round off the corners as accurately as possible. Much practice is needed for these operations before you gain control of your hands and are able to make the exact shape you want. Fig. 55 shows how a small bevel is first ground round the base. This is to strengthen the edges.

Fig 66 Applying powder to buff

DOPPING

The first stage being completed, the stone must now be dopped. This consists of cementing it onto a handling stick (a piece of small-gauge dowelling, a pencil or a nail may be used), to give more control when shaping, and also so that more pressure can be exerted. Prepared dop sticks may be bought at a lapidary shop, but it is very simple to make your own. Have a supply of dop sticks, in various sizes, and some dopping wax.

Obtain a tripod, with a bunsen burner or spirit lamp as heating agent, and warm the dopping wax over this in a crucible or heat-proof ladle until it is melted to bubbling point. Dip the dop stick into the wax and circle around, allowing layer on layer to form a good blob on the end. Mould the wax evenly onto the stick, to give adequate support to the stone, and then shape the top into a conical form roughly to fit the shape of the stone. Now put an asbestos mat over the flame, place the stone on it, and warm it gradually. At the same time reheat the dopstick – both the stone and the wax should be of the same temperature when being attached to each other, and quite hot at the moment of joining, if a good bond is to be

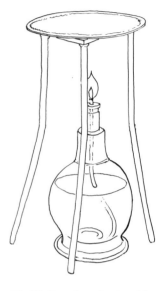

Fig 57 Dopping tripod and burner

Fig 58 Dopstick being dipped

70

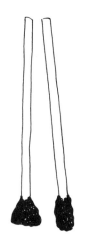

Fig 59 Moulding the wax

made. Do not use too much wax, or the marking on the base of the cabochon will be covered.

Attach the dop quickly and carefully onto the back of the stone while it is still on the asbestos mat, so that it can be lifted off and placed on the bench. Mould the wax around the stone while the wax is warm. Re-heat if necessary. When a good union has been made, set aside on a metal plate to cool.

It is more practical and time-saving to do all your dopping at the same time. So if you have other stones to polish, they can all be dopped simultaneously. Figs 57–61 illustrate dopping.

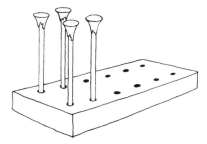

Fig 60 Stand for dopsticks

Fig 61 Attaching and centring

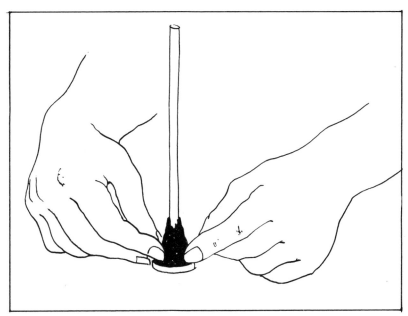

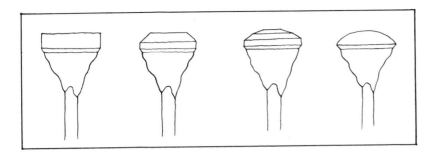

Fig 62 Grinding steep bevel

GRINDING THE TOP

Use the rough grinding wheel with grit, usually No. 120, and proceed as follows: switch on motor and turn on water. Always do these two operations in this order, and be sure to turn off the water *before* the wheel is stopped. The first step here is to grind a steep bevel around the edges of the stone, sloping from the base to the top at an angle of approximately 25° (fig. 62). This is to widen the cabochon at the bottom, so that its setting may be secure. Hold the dopped stone in the left hand close to its base, and rock with the right hand, making a roughly-cut bevel around the circumference of the stone. Both hands should be steadying, but the right hand should also be rocking the dopped stone, making continuous narrow cuts at each turn of the stick until the bevel reaches the base of the cabochon but *not* beyond (figs 63–65). Several bevels may be necessary to rough out the preliminary shape, and you must always guard against the tendency to work on a small section rather than on the whole. The symmetry of the outline must always be the first consideration, and your care in the early shaping of the dome will be well worth the trouble. The basic form must be correct before you start to smooth out the rougher edges. At all costs avoid the beginner's fault of flattening the dome too much at the top. Continually check, by holding it sideways to observe the shape in cross-section. Wash, dry, and inspect again before the next step.

Fig 63 Stage 1, grinding the stone

Fig 64 Stage 2, grinding the stone

Fig 65 Stage 3, grinding the stone

FINE GRINDING

A No. 200-grit wheel is used for this, turning at the same speed, with water as a coolant. Go over the entire surface of the stone, using a lighter but still firm pressure, and keeping it in continuous movement. The aim now is to remove the deeper scratches, until a smooth finish is obtained. Clean and inspect regularly, and mark with aluminium pencil the areas that need retouching. Avoid burn spots, which will be seen when the stone is dry, and are generally caused either by lack of water or too much pressure, so that the stone becomes over-heated. These patches must be removed before sanding, should they occur.

SANDING

Usually two or more stages of sanding must be done – a coarse and a finer one – and these may be carried out on a horizontal or a vertical wheel.

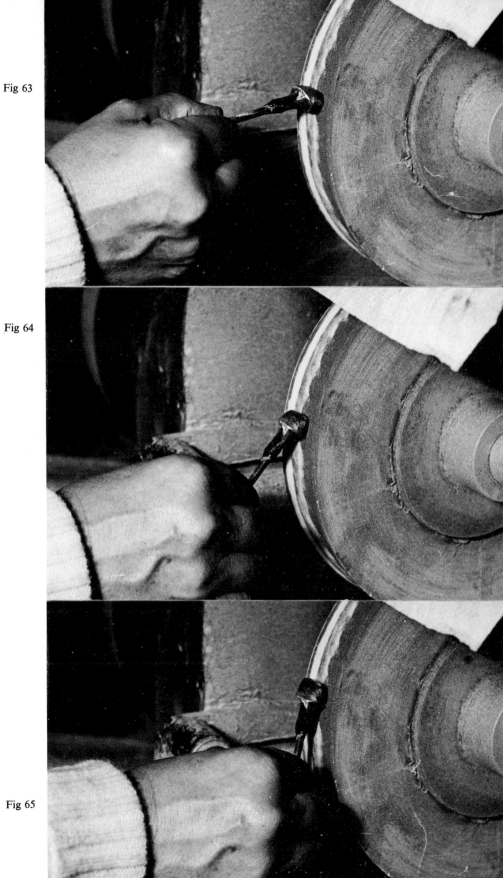

Fig 63

Fig 64

Fig 65

Wet sanding is preferable to dry, as the abrasive action is better, removing the deeper scratches more successfully, and the stone is less likely to become over-heated.

To make the agate cabochon, a vertical wheel is being used, of No. 400 grit for the coarse sanding and No. 600 to 800 for the final sanding. Both should run at a speed of 2400 rpm. Again the water drip is a necessity. Manipulate the stone on the No. 450 carborundum wheel until all scratches are removed. Wash carefully, checking that all the grit has been cleared off before changing it onto the second sanding wheel.

Work on this one in a similar manner, with a No. 600 to 800 grit, until a fine glossy polish is revealed, with only minute scratches visible. The cabochon should now barely clear the template shape when tested against it.

POLISHING

Mix a small quantity of polishing powder thinly with water – cerium oxide or tin oxide are commonly used – preparing only enough for the day's work. This is applied to the revolving wheel with a soft-haired brush in as small amounts as can be absorbed by the polishing belt, known as the 'buff' (fig. 66). Wheels with leather buffs are the most common, but felt is also used.

Adjust the wheel to run at a lower speed, about 750 rpm, and switch on the motor. It is difficult to estimate the amount of pressure needed. Even when the sanding has been adequate, considerable pressure is often needed to bring up a good polish (fig. 67). Much depends on the type of stone you are polishing, and you will only learn by experience. Beware of drying out the buff and over-heating the stone by excessive pressure.

Start with the bevel, as in the previous operations, and work round into the top as before, continuing until a mirror-like polish is achieved – it should be possible to see the reflection from an electric light bulb on any part of the surface.

Now remove the stone from the dopstick, by melting the wax gently over low heat, holding the stone with a cloth while prising it off. Clean off any wax with methylated spirits. It may also be removed by dipping in iced water.

It may be necessary to flatten and polish the base further, if you are working on a transparent or translucent stone. For the agate, a flat base is the only requirement.

The finished stone is now ready for mounting or exhibiting

Points on cutting and polishing

SAWING

The stone can be held close against the diamond saw blade without fear of cutting yourself. Diamond blades will cut through rock, but will not cut you.

Fig 67 Polishing stone against buff

Fig 68 All the stages of cabochon making

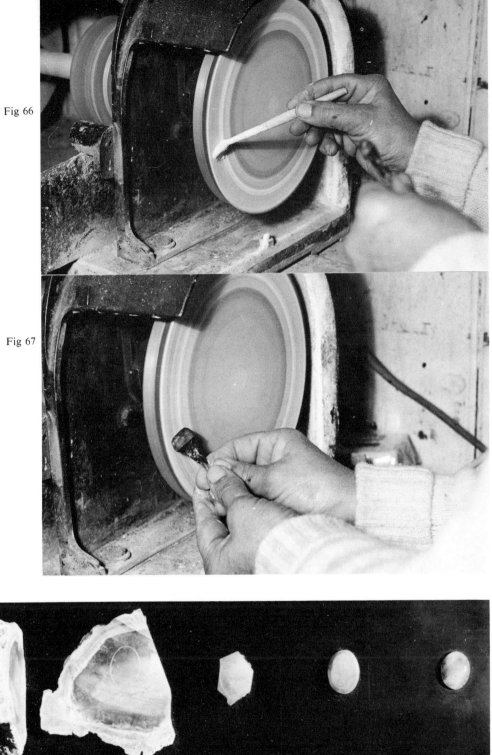

Fig 66

Fig 67

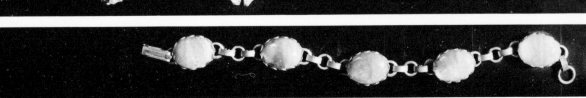

UNDERCUTTING

This is a common problem during sanding, and should be explained. Some stones are a combination of different minerals of diverse structure, with a tendency to be weak in some directions and harder in others. This applies more to rocks than gemstones, obviously, but in all cases this difference in grain shows up in sanding and polishing, causing the weaker parts to wear away faster. Because of this the surface of the stone is left pitted and mottled, with a rather bumpy appearance. Banded stones are often badly affected.

Sometimes a higher rpm improves the situation, but on the whole it is better to avoid stones with this tendency to undercut. Another method of avoiding undercutting is to paint the stone with Araldite and allow this to harden before polishing, to cover pits and soft patches.

It is advisable to wear a magnifying visor while you are working on a stone, so that the most minute cracks and flaws will be visible.

Never leave the grinding or sanding wheels standing in water. Drain off immediately after use.

DOPPING

Never let the wax over-run the marking line.

8 What to do with stones

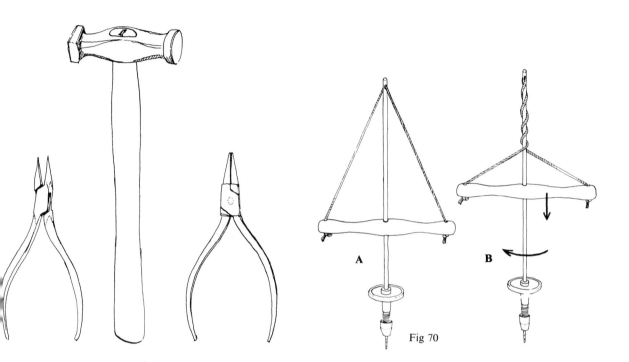

Fig 69 Planishing hammer, pliers

Fig 70 Jewelry drill. A. stationary.
B. showing twisting action

The first thought that comes to mind regarding gemstones is their use in fine jewelry, in settings of gold and silver. I do not propose to discuss the techniques of fine jewelry-making and the craft of the silversmith in this book; they are subjects in themselves. If you become interested in setting your stones, you should go on to study design and techniques at a lapidary class, or from a book dealing with the subject.

If, however, you are content to set your cabochons and baroques in simple settings, these can be bought from most lapidary suppliers, who have wide selections of jewelry findings (mounts) for making rings, brooches, necklaces, pendants, cuff-links, bracelets, earrings, key-rings and other things (figs 71–80). They are usually available in plated gold, silver, or in stainless steel; and your own stones are simply attached to the findings with an epoxy cement such as Araldite or Unistick. Most findings are well and simply designed; the procedure for attaching the stones is very simple, with instructions included by the firm supplying the findings. They should stress the importance of making sure that no grease of any sort comes into contact with the stones and the findings when they are joined – even the natural oil in the finger tip can affect the union.

Tumbled stones of all sorts are popular for simple jewelry making. Finer specimens which have been cut and polished by hand deserve special attention when you are considering their setting, but most of the commercial findings (mountings) are well designed and very adequate for the job. Avoid the more ornate types, as they may detract from the quality and character of the stones.

The few tools that you will require for this work are as follows: a planishing hammer, small pliers (preferably chain-nose), see fig. 69, a jewelry drill (fig. 70), silver shears about 7 ins long (not illustrated), a length of sterling silver wire (14 to 16 Brown and Sharp gauge) and sheet silver (22 B and S gauge). Most of these will be required for making the jewelry described later.

A list of some of the most commonly used findings (mountings) follows, with short descriptions of their uses.

Jump rings

Split rings made in various sizes used as connecting links to join other sections, such as bell caps (see below) or to link earring fittings. They should be chosen in sizes appropriate for their purpose (fig. 71).

Bell caps

A claw type holder made in several designs and sizes, which is cemented to the stone with an adhesive of the epoxy resin type. A jump ring is linked to the ring at the top of the bell cap. Choose one of the right size and type for your stone. See fig. 72 for two examples.

Ear fittings (earwires – mountings)

There are many varieties of these. The following describes some of them:
Screw-on fittings (mountings): with ring for dangles, or concave plate for cementing stones (fig. 73B).
Fittings (mountings): with plate for cementing stone for stud earrings, available with clips or ear-pins. Butterfly fitting for pierced ears – see fig. 73C.
Pierce earwires: for dangling stones for pierced ears. Here the stone (or stones) are attached by jump ring and bell cap (fig. 73A).

Rings

Rings for cabochon stones with concave pads, made in several depths and adjustable sizes (fig. 74A). Rings for cabochons, with oval pad setting (mounting) or plain adjustable (fig. 74B). Rings with adjustable claw fittings to take cabochons, baroques or rough mineral specimens (fig. 74C).

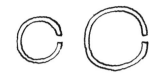

Fig 71   Jump rings

Fig 72   Bell caps

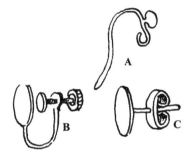

Fig 73 Ear fittings. A. pierce earwires B. screw-on fittings. C. fittings for studs

Fig 74 Rings. A. for cabochons with concave pads. B. for cabochons with oval pad settings. C. adjustable claw fitting

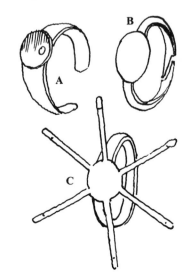

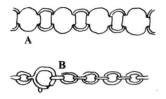

A

B

Fig 75 Bracelets. A. with pads for cementing flat based stones. B. chain bracelet for dangling stones

Fig 76 Pendants. A. holder setting for round, square or flat stones. B. holder setting with frilled or fancy edges. C. claw holder for cabochons or flat-based stones

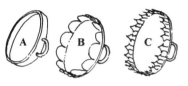

Fig 77 Necklets. Flat trace chains

Bracelets

Bracelets with round or square pads for cementing flat-based stones (fig. 75A). Chain bracelets for dangling stones attached to bell caps (fig. 75B). Bracelets with pads alternating with intertwined link chain, for use with flat-based stones and dangling tumbled stones. Bracelets with pads for cementing cabochons with plain, frilled or fancy settings. In several sizes.

Note: In making both bracelets and necklets the size is decided by the number of links used, and when bought in lengths you simply cut off the required amount, adding or removing links to adjust the fit.

Pendants

Holder setting (mounting) for round, square or flat stones (fig. 76A). Holder setting (mounting) with frilled or fancy edges (fig. 76B). Claw holder (mounting) for cabochons or flat-based mineral specimens (fig. 76C). All pendant settings come in various sizes.

Necklets

Flat trace chains with bolt rings to attach stones mounted on bell caps (fig. 77). Rope chain with bolt rings and innumerable other types of chain are available, and are sold by the metre.

Brooches

Rectangular pinbacks sold in varied lengths for attaching a single or a row of stones. Pinbacks with round, oval or square pads for cementing stones (fig. 78A). Irregularly-shaped pinbacks for baroques (fig. 78B). Brooch fob for drops. Four-prong moulded brooch base – several mm. sizes to fit most shapes of stones. Many varieties of fancy settings: see fig. 78C for twisted gold mount.

Fig 78 Brooches. A. pinbacks with round, oval or square pads. B. irregularly-shaped pinbacks for baroques. C. twisted or fancy settings

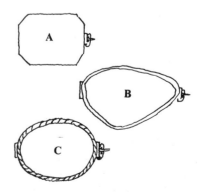

Cuff links

Plain moulded settings (mountings) in various sizes. Fig. 79B, frilled and fancy settings in varied shapes and sizes, fig. 79A, flat and concave pad settings in many sizes. Claw settings (mountings) for round or oval cabochons.

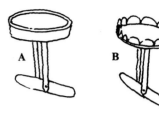

Fig 79 Cuff links. A. plain moulded settings for cuff links. B. frilled and fancy settings for cuff links

Key rings

Ring with chain and jump ring for attaching stones on bell cap (fig. 80A). Ring with separate links. Baroques and pebbles may be attached by bell cap and extra jump ring.

Fig 80 Key rings. A. key ring with chain and jump ring. B. key ring with separate links

Two examples of simple but arresting hand-made earrings are included for those who prefer to work directly from the basic materials, rather than from findings (mountings). They were designed by the Hawaiian artist-jeweller Barbara Engels in sterling silver, hand-beaten with a planishing hammer. Briefly, this is how they were constructed:

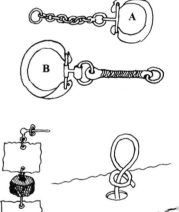

Fig. 81: two squares of $\frac{3}{4}$-inch silver and a small rectangle were cut out of silver (22 B and S gauge). After cutting to shape they were hammered, giving the typically serrated edge, thus enlarging the area. Two holes were drilled in each of the larger rectangles (see fig. 70 for drill) and one in the smaller one, to take the links. The three silver units for each earring were linked together with silver twisted wire, but the amateur could use jump rings. The jade bead suspended between the two squares was joined by silver wire, 14 B and S gauge. See fig. 82 for the twist knot in the wire. A pierce earwire fitting was attached.

Fig. 83: the silver sheet and wire were of the same gauges as used in fig. 81, also the earwire fitting. A circle of about $\frac{3}{4}$-inch diameter was cut out of the silver sheet and a hole drilled in the centre. The disc was then beaten until it was approximately one inch in diameter. Two skilfully-twisted spirals of wire were dangled from the base of the silver disc through drilled holes. These could be omitted. An amber bead was linked between the earwire ring and the disc. For both types of earrings all rough edges must be filed smooth, first with a needle file and then with emery paper. Note that both have a butterfly fitting on the earwire.

Fig 81   Earrings in beaten silver squares

Fig 82 Diagram of wire twist knot

Fig 83 Earring in beaten silver with amber head

Tumbled stones, especially of the translucent varieties, will be popular for jewelry of this sort; but the more humble beach pebbles, which may be tumbled in quantities, can be stacked in bowls, set on tables and window-ledges, until one wonders what else can be done with them. The following suggestions apply equally well to natural stones – unpolished, but of pleasing or arresting textures.

Fig 84 Rings showing cabochon-cuts and rough crystal, by David Pearce

Fig 85 Pendants showing imaginative settings, by David Pearce

opposite
Fig 89 Necklace pendants of rose quartz and rough crystal, by David Pearce

Fig 86 Tumbled agate set as pendant for necklace, by Klares Lewes

Fig 87 Fortification agate set as pendant, by Klares Lewes

Fig 88 View of complete pendant, showing agate, by Klares Lewes

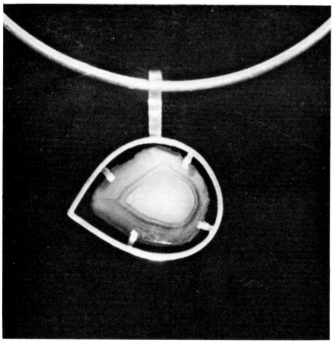

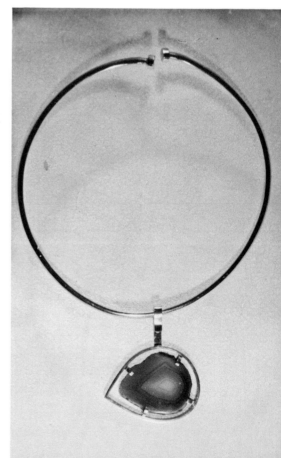

opposite
Fig 91   Stones on conservatory staging. Courtesy J. Ede

Fig 92   Sculptural stones. Courtesy J. Ede

Fig 93   Natural stones on cane platter. Courtesy J. Ede

Fig 90 Polished pebbles in jar

Heap a handful of pebbles around the base of house plants. Or use pebbles to line troughs or containers for plants, to provide moisture and drainage. If you have some larger stones, natural or polished, they may be placed at random over a greenhouse staging or window sill between pot plants (fig. 91).

Some of the illustrations will perhaps give you further ideas for displaying your stones and pebbles.

Fig. 92 shows a group of natural stones so sculptural in character that they resemble a bronze casting. They have such an obvious degree of tactility that one wants to handle them.

Fig. 93 shows on a flat cane platter a carefully chosen group of natural stones, sorted from beach shingle, and graded in colour from dense black through the range of greys to scintillating white quartzite.

Fig. 95 is a further example of sorted natural stones, this time graded by size into a spiral design. Again the shades are neutral – dark grey, pale grey, to white.

Fig 91

Fig 92

Fig 93

Fig 94 Wire holder soldered on stand for exhibiting crystals

Fig 95 Stones in spiral arrangement

In order to mount arrangements such as these, you will need quite a large collection from which to select. If you can spend unlimited time on shingle beaches, search on a rota system for the best results. For example, reserve a morning for collecting only black stones of good proportion. On another day pick up only grey, or white, or red, or brown. Alternatively you may choose to collect by size or by shape – ovoids, globes, cylinders, pear shapes, possibly irregularly shaped flints, or those with cavities enclosing little pebbles.

Even when you are collecting neutral-coloured material, choose a bright sunny day if possible, and always check the depth of colour by dipping them in water. Searching for carnelians is an art in itself. A sunny day is essential, and you must walk towards the sun, preferably along a wet stretch of shore, where the brilliant glow of this lovely stone will strike out like a flame from the monochrome of the shingle. The experts say that it takes nearly an hour to 'get your eye in' and begin to see carnelians; and one person can search patiently for half a day and possibly find two, while another will find forty in the same time on the same stretch of shore.

You may buy large slabs of material such as jasper, serpentine, porphyritic granite, oolitic limestone, agatized wood or the unlimited varieties of agate, for slicing either with a slab saw or a trim saw. These make impressive bookends when cut to uniform size and polished on a lap.

If you wish to collect and display natural specimens, such as fine crystals, or translucent slabbed sections, the following idea might appeal to you. Use a window as a show case if your view is uninteresting or ugly. The clear glass is removed and obscured glass fitted in its place. Steel slotted strips are built into the sides of the window, and glass shelving fitted. This can be cased in clear glass, built over the front as in double glazing, or left as ordinary shelving – whichever you prefer. Strip lighting may be fitted above or at the sides, to enhance the sparkle of crystals and the scintillation of other specimens. Opaque minerals such as geodes and nodules and thunder eggs may also be displayed.

Exhibiting stones in a synthetic resin base is another effective way of showing them off. This method may be used for a small table top, or for the setting of one or more perfect specimens – such as a delicately patterned agate section.

The technique is not difficult, and basically consists of embedding the stones in a transparent substance which will finally set glass-hard Several commercially-manufactured products are available, and in the example described below Bondaglass is used.

This resin is supplied with a catalyst, which is added immediately before use, and the solution poured over the stone arrangement. After a certain period, depending on temperature, the substance 'cures' (sets hard), becoming quite hot during this process. Embedding stones to make a flat plaque requires the pouring of several layers of resin, and each one must set glass-hard before being covered by the next layer. The curing is faster in higher temperatures, and is sometimes carried out in a warming cupboard.

A containing mould is required for the operation, and this may be made of plaster, wood, hardboard or acetate sheets, sealed together as an open-topped box. Wood or plaster moulds must be coated with a release agent (supplied by the manufacturers), so that the resin mould can be released easily when it has set. The actual thickness of the stones dictates the depth of the mould – they require a preliminary bed of resin of about $\frac{1}{4}$-in. thickness to settle on, and a final top covering of the same depth.

As there is often shrinking while the resin is curing, large amounts are obviously more difficult to control than smaller ones, so it is better to make a start with something quite modest. Choose some small mineral that will fit into a tin or a lid, and use this as the mould, first coating it with the release agent or vaseline, thinly smeared.

Pour in the resin solution in a thin layer, in which to bed the stones. Arrange them when it becomes tacky, and allow to harden. Then pour in successive layers of the solution, which must be freshly mixed each time, until the stones are covered, the final layer filling the mould to the rim. Place a sheet of glass or acetate coated with release agent over it, ensuring that it actually touches the resin. This excludes the air from inhibiting the setting on the top face. If you fail to make direct contact between the glass and the resin, a tacky, frosted surface will result, which will require filling, scraping and polishing.

Fig 96 Resin mould, showing glass placed over the top

Two further points must be noted: porous stones should first be painted with the resin, or small air bubbles will develop around them. Should any of these appear and rise to the surface, they should be pricked and gently brushed off towards the edge of the mould.

Firms marketing synthetic resins should supply a book of instructions about the use of their particular product. These should be followed carefully, as the procedure may vary.

Another manner of displaying stones in table top form is to use slabbed sections taken from material of distinctive pattern, such as orbicular jasper, turritella, agate, conglomerate, breccia or agatized wood. They should be sawn to a uniform thickness and the entire surface covered as completely as possible. Have plenty of material to hand from which to select while you are arranging the design, keeping it well within the confines of your chosen base. Extras you will require are:

An adhesive such as Unistick or Araldite.

Tile cement for grouting (infilling between the slabs to give a smooth level surface).

Spatula for spreading the tile cement.

Plate glass $\frac{3}{4}$ in. thick (optional).

Suitable edging to surround.

Blockboard on $\frac{1}{2}$-in. plywood base.

If you prefer to make a tray instead of a table, the slabs must be as thin as possible or it will be too heavy to carry around, but if the weight is immaterial the slabs can be thicker.

Experiment with the arrangement of the material until you have

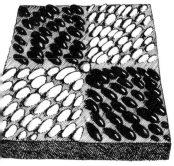

ig 97 Design for pebble section for
aving

g 98 Design for pebble section for
ving

g 99 Flint pavement

decided on the design and then, using the adhesive, attach the slices to the base. Place a weighted board on the top and leave until the slices are well stuck. The time this will take depends on the adhesive you use, but make sure all are firm before you start infilling.

Mix the tile cement and lay it into all the spaces between the slabs, using the spatula to spread and force it down, so that no spaces or cracks are left unfilled and you have a uniformly even surface. Great care must be taken at this grouting stage in not allowing the cement to run over the polished surface of the stones. Where this happens, as it inevitably will, wipe off quickly before it dries.

It may be difficult to achieve a perfectly flat finish at your first attempt. Until you are experienced in sawing, the slabs are apt to vary in thickness. If this presents a problem, cover the whole area with a sheet of plate glass and attach an appropriate edging strip. Before doing this, however, be sure that the entire surface is polished clean up to the edges. This should result in a very striking patterned surface of polished stones with the infilling of cement giving a smooth flat finish. Ordinary building cement can be used in place of tile cement, but if later you should want to remove any section, the tile cement is less hard. Both may be tinted with a cement colourant, if you want a toned background.

Outdoor use of pebbles

From the earliest times stones and pebbles have been used decoratively to make patterns on streets, floors, courtyards and walls. People in such widely differing places as China, Spain, Mexico, Rome and Greece have used this enduring medium to embellish ground areas and the sides of buildings.

It is still possible to lay your own pavement, working the separate areas over a period of time. Two different methods are available. The first one involves the making of pre-formed pebble-inlaid blocks which can be of any shape you wish (figs 97, 98). In the second, the pebbles are laid directly into wet cement *in situ*, the units being separated by paving stones, blocks, tiles, bricks or prefabricated forms.

METHOD 1

Decide on the shape for your block and make a framework – of wood if it is to be removable, or in a rustless metal strip if it is to remain as a retaining wall. The frame is then placed on a blockwood board and held in place with nails around the outside. An area of reinforcing wire is cut to fit within an inch of the edge of the frame, to give stability.

Make a mortar of one part of cement to three parts of sand. Trowel this mix into the frame and level with a flat stick before marking out the design idea for placing the pebbles. Use a sharp stick for drawing the lines on the mortar, which should be firm and fairly stiff.

Lay in the pebbles on these design lines, working from the centre outwards and as quickly as possible. Leave for several days to set. Points to observe:

1   Choose units of a size that you can cover with pebbles within the setting time of the mortar. Do an experimental block before you mix the mortar.

2   If you collect a supply of mixed pebbles over the summer months to build up a reserve, you can make pebble plaques during the winter, working indoors in a prepared frame.

3   Design points to be observed are that pebbles used for area groups should be of uniform shape (such as ovoid, spherical, etc.), size and colour, to give form and contrast to the pattern. Strongly contrasting tones like black and white are the most effective (see fig. 97).

4   The pebbles can be angled, laid on edge, or placed flat. The latter position is not advised, as they tend to sink into the mortar when pressed down and become partially obscured. In all cases, they should be bedded down well by hammering gently with a wooden mallet until they are about two-thirds down in the mortar.

5   Always group the materials closely together. If you have not sufficient pebbles for this, leave an area of plain cement rather than a sparsely-patterned one.

METHOD 2

This is for setting either pebble units or singly placed pebbles between other units, such as bricks, concrete slabs or paving stones.

The site for the pavement should be measured and pegged out with a line of string to surround it. It should be levelled (using a spirit level), and a layer of coarse aggregate laid, usually $\frac{1}{2}$ in. gravel. This should be allowed to settle before the cement is laid.

The paving slabs, bricks or whatever you intend to use between the pebble units should now be laid. Work on small areas at a time.

Prepare a mortar of three parts sand to one part cement and trowel this into the spaces left between the other units. Into this set the prepared slabs or press in the individual pebbles, whichever you have previously decided on. Bed down well by placing a board over the top and hammering with a mallet. Proceed section by section, further areas being laid when the previous ones have set. On starting each new part, wet the dry mortar thoroughly before trowelling in the new lot.

Many variations are possible within these techniques, and the same treatment can be applied to other surfaces – walls, the base of pools, or for decorative areas indoors. Polished stones also are very impressive used in these projects.

An example of knapped flint paving is illustrated (fig. 99). These flints came from Grimes Graves Quarries, at Brandon in Norfolk, where the ancient craft of flint-knapping is still carried out, though now a dying art. The offcuts for this pavement were purchased there.

It may appear in this book that too much attention is paid to the unpretentious pebble, and that lapidary should be concerned only with gemstones and semi-precious stones. The actual definition of 'lapidary' is 'concerned with stones', although the second definition states 'cutter', polisher or engraver of gems'. And beautiful pebbles are easily available to everyone, so the interpretation is justified; and is developed and expanded in this book to cover interest in both fields.

Specific gravity table

Amber	1.07	Fluor	3.18
Jet	1.32	Spodumene	3.18
Opal	2.10	Jadeite	3.33
Obsidian	2.40	Olivine	3.34
Serpentine	2.55	Epidote	3.40
Chalcedony	2.61	Rhodonite	3.53
Quartz	2.65	Topaz	3.54
Feldspar	2.65	Labradorite	3.70
Beryl	2.70	Garnet (grossular)	3.70
Calcite	2.71	Rhodochrosite	3.70
Pearl	2.71	Chrysoberyl	3.71
Turquoise	2.80	Malachite	3.80
Lapis lazuli	2.80	Azurite	3.83
Nephrite	2.96	Pyrites	4.93
Tourmaline	3.06		

Agate
Carnelian

Marble
Serpentine

Garnets

Contin

Portsoy

Amethyst
Garnets
Cairngorm

Cairngorm Mts

Cairngorm

Glen Tilt

Garnets

Montrose

Agate
Amethyst
Cairngorm

Tiree

Garnets

Iona

Jasper
Campsie Glen

Garnets

Agate
Carnelian

Cairngorm
Amethyst

Largs
Amethyst
Irvine

Leadhills

Pentland Hills

Agate
Carnelian

Sandstone
Holy Island

Carnelian
Agate

Aragonite
Cairngorm

Dalbeattie

Fluorspar
Alston
Weardale
Dufton

Jet

Sandstone
Agate
Carnelian
Amber
Limestone

Mourne Mts

Beryl
Aquamarine

St Bees
Egremont

Agate
Jasper
Chalcedony

Calcite
Barite

Whitby

Scarborough

Flint

Sandstone
Milky Quartz
Chalcedony
Agate
Carnelian
Jet
Amber
Jasper

Connemara Mts

Marble

Quartzite
Gabbro
Mica Schist
Granite
Serpentine
Sandstone

Green Schist
Jasper

Agate
Schist

Granite
Limestone
Sandstone

Snowdon

Milky Quartz

Castleton

Blue John
Fluorspar

Flint

Cromer

Good pebble coast

Felixstowe

Dolerite

St Brides Bay

Sandstone
Quartzite
Limestone

Limestone

Agate

Clevedon
Churchill

Deal

Rhodonite

Milton Abbot

Sidmouth

Chert

Agate

Breccia

Hastings
Eastbourne

Quartz
Carnelian

Flint
Sandstone

Cairngorm
Citrine
Amethyst
Serpentine
Rose Quartz
Granite
Slate
Chalcedony
Jasper
Agate
Carnelian
Quartz

Serpentine
Gneiss
Schist
Gabbro
Quartz

Slate
Schist
Granite
Dolerite
Sandstone
Quartzite

Limestone
Sandstone
Slate
Dolerite

Flint
Limestone
Chert
Quartzite
Jasper
Granite

Jasper
Quartz

Sandstone
Limestone

Quartzite
Chert

Granite
Quartz

Localities

British Isles Coastal areas

KENT
Sandwich and Deal. Pebbles of quartz and chalcedony, flints and flint nodules
Folkestone. Ammonite fossils, mother-of-pearl coated, are found in the cliffs

SUSSEX
Bexhill, Hastings and Fairlight. Pebbles of quartzite, chert, varied coloured flints

ISLE OF WIGHT
Most beaches from Culvar Cliff to Luccombe—quartz varieties including rock
   crystal, agate, carnelian, sardonyx, jasper, agate geodes

DORSET
Chesil Beach. Stretching for eighteen miles, this beach provides fine grade
   pebbles of flint, chert, limestone, jasper and quartzite
Abbotsbury. Agate, carnelian
Purbeck. Fine variety of marble
Lyme Regis. Ammonite fossils coated with gold pyrites embedded in cliffs

DEVON
Budleigh Salterton to Langstone Point. Fine breccia and conglomerate, attractive
   pebbles to cut and polish
Dart Estuary and Start Point. A run of shingle beaches of great interest. Sandstone,
   green schist, red and blue slate, dolerite, quartzite and agate fairly abundant
Prawle Point. Green schist, mica schist, finely veined with quartz occurring in
   metamorphic rocks
Newton Abbot. Rhodonite

CORNWALL
St Michael's Mount and Marazion Beach. One of the best localities in Cornwall.
   Pale blue topaz, garnet (massive), agate, carnelian, jasper, moss agate, chryso-
   prase, opal, rose quartz, citrine, amethyst, serpentine—all in pebble form
Penzance. Many of the above varieties
Lizard. Fine green serpentine, also red and black. Calcite, feldspar
St Agnes to Perranporth at Cligga Head. Pegmatites, and disused mines with gold
   quartz veins, small topaz crystals, tourmaline

West Coast of England

PEMBROKESHIRE
Saundersfoot. Shingle beach which was a dumping ground for ballast in the
   nineteenth century. Now has a great variety of pebbles from outside localities

St Bride's Bay. Sandstone, quartzite, limestone, interspersed among the volcanic rocks

Cemmaes Head. Agate and jasper

MERIONETH
Dolgellau. Pyrites, gold-bearing quartz

ANGLESEY
Coastline. Abundance of varied material. Jasper, green schist, mica schist, sandstone, dolerite, gabbro, serpentine, agate

Parys Mountains. Quartz, pyrites

CUMBERLAND
St Bee's Head, Fleswick Bay. Jasper, carnelian, agate, quartz varieties, chalcedony, many fine multi-coloured pebbles for tumbling. Beach inaccessible at high tide

East Coast of England

The Northumberland coast has many stretches of mixed pebbles with limestone and shale predominating, also interesting sandstone. Between the Tyne Estuary and Hartlepool, yellow limestone

YORKSHIRE
Whitby (Jet Rock). Jet, occasionally amber

Whitby to Flamborough Head. Agate, carnelian, amber, limestone, sandstone, citrine, flint

Scarborough. Banded agate

Filey Bay. Oolitic limestone

NORFOLK
Blakeney Point to Cromer. Chalcedony in many varieties, agate, carnelian (noted for this), jasper, quartzite, milky quartz, amber, jet, flint, sandstone. Some of the fine shingle beaches are ideal for collecting pebble varieties for polishing.

SUFFOLK
Felixstowe and Aldeburgh. Chalcedony varieties, carnelian, jasper, jet, agate, flint, sandstone and quartzite

Inland England

SURREY
Nutfield. Yellow barite geodes lined with quartz

DEVON
Oakehampton (Meldon Quarry). Green and pink tourmaline crystals

CORNWALL
Camborne. The School of Mines should be visited. It has a fine collection of locally available minerals

Redruth-Camborne area. Apatite, calcite, mica, chalcedony, red jasper, garnet, pale green fluorite, malachite (Basset Mines)

Callington. Mines in surrounding hills, especially Wheal St Mary. Malachite, azurite, chrysocolla, fluorite crystals, tourmaline

SOMERSET
Bridgwater (Ben Combe). Malachite

Shiplake in Loxton. Fine agate geodes

Mendip Hills. Calcite, barite, haematite

Cheddar. Orbicular agate

GLOUCESTERSHIRE
Yate. Celestite, barite
Bristol area. Landscape marble, rhodochrosite
Clifton. Quartz
Forest of Dean. Haematite

LEICESTERSHIRE
Charnwood Forest area. Road metal quarries produce small amounts of epidote, jasper, chalcedony. Other quarries in igneous region provide azurite, malachite.

CAERNARVON
Mt Snowdon. Milky quartz

DERBYSHIRE
Castleton. Fluorite (blue john variety), barite, calcite
Crich. Fluorite, pink and green banded barite. Brown barite (oakstone), excellent for slabbing and polishing

CO. DURHAM
Weardale. Fluorite
Fulwell. Magnesium limestone
Boltsburn Mine. Fluorite

CUMBERLAND
Egremont. Calcite
Carrock Fell. Green apatite, feldspar, various pyrites and other more rare minerals
Keswick area (*Roughton Gill mine dumps*). Malachite, naematite
Skiddaw Mountains. Fine andalusite crystals in dark hornsfelsed rocks

WESTMORLAND
Shap. Andalusite crystals. Pink and grey porphyritic granite and other minerals in works on west side of Shap Village
Blue Shap Quarry. Epidote in veins. Pink garnet in good crystals abundant in walls and spoil heaps

Scotland

AYRSHIRE
Dunure. Agate, carnelian
Larga. Amethyst
Ballantrae. Serpentine

KIRKUDBRIGHT
Dalbeattie. Cairngorm
Kippford (*Needles Eye*). Amethyst pebbles in streams
Glenburn (*New Abbey*). Amethyst pebbles in streams

LANARKSHIRE
Leadhills. Haematite, quartz, calcite

MIDLOTHIAN
Pentland Hills (near Carlops). Agate, carnelian

EAST LOTHIAN
Haddington (on River Tyne). Agate, carnelian varieties
Dunbar Beach. Agate, carnelian, chalcedony varieties

ISLE OF ARRAN (BUTESHIRE)
Rosa Burn. Sapphire (spindle-shaped crystals), amethyst

Brodick to Machrie (south of String). Sandstone, conglomerate, breccia, obsidian, porphyry, gabbro
Old Red Sandstone area. Jasper, carnelian, milk opal, agate
Goatfell area. Topaz, beryl, garnet (alamandine), tourmaline

KINTYRE (ARGYLLSHIRE)
Campbelltown. Amethyst, cairngorm.

JURA AND IONA (ARGYLLSHIRE)
Garnet, Serpentine

STIRLING
Campsie Glen. Jasper

FIFESHIRE
Elie Ness. Garnets widely distributed
Luthrie (hills around). Cairngorm
Firth of Tay (shores). Agate, carnelian

PERTHSHIRE
Glen Tilt. Serpentine, garnet
Ochil Hills. Agate, carnelian
Path of Condie. Agate, carnelian

ANGUS
Usan. Amethyst in agate nodules, carnelian, agate, cairngorm
Montrose, Ferryden, Scurdie Ness. Chalcedony varieties, agate, carnelian

CAIRNGORM MOUNTAINS
A rich source for many varieties of quartz and chalcedony. Consult Regional Geological Survey Maps. Gem-hunting courses are run by the Scottish Council of Physical Recreation at Glenmore Lodge

BANFFSHIRE
Portsoy. Serpentine, marble. Fine pebble beach
River Avon area (mountains and streams). Good smoky quartz

ROSS AND CROMARTY
Garve (hills above). Garnet (alamandine), amethyst, cairngorm
Ardmair Bay (*near Ullapool*). Agate, carnelian

SUTHERLAND
Ben More Assynt (near Lochinver). Outcrops of pink gneiss, dark hornblende gneiss, garnet
Glen Dunrobin. Amethyst, smoky quartz
Kylisku, Scourie. Serpentine

North America

The collecting of gem material in the USA and Canada is a hobby with over three million enthusiasts, some enjoying it simply for the thrill of collecting, while others hope to find good specimens for lapidary work. A large section buy rough minerals from suppliers to work on.

The lapidary movement has developed in North America to an extent far beyond that found in other countries. Although Australia and Southern Africa, both comparably rich in mineral deposits, are collecting with increasing enthusiasm, the USA is still an unrivalled field for the 'rock hound'.

Today, many of the former gem areas are barred to the public, being now either privately or state-owned, but it is the general custom to allow collecting on payment of a small fee. You should find out beforehand what rules and conditions prevail and then approach the owner for the necessary permission.

Most private land in the east is now barred to the collector, but in the west there are still vast areas owned by the us Government which are public property and open to the 'rock hound'. This part of the country is climatically favourable all the year round; geographically, conditions are ideal for the formation of quartz gems and agate, stemming as it does from a volcanically active past.

So although the whole continent is rich in minerals, the western half is the best hunting ground, extending from the jade of Alaska and Wyoming, sapphires of Montana, to the turquoise of Nevada and New Mexico. California is the richest state of all for its variety of gemstones, especially the quartz family, but the main source of agate is in Oregon where there are several famous localities. The renowned Oregon thunder egg from the Fulton Agate Beds is one of the prizes from this area.

A very brief mention should be made of some of the most rewarding sites, and it is proposed to deal with the two states most richly endowed with minerals— Oregon and California. To cover all the states a large book could be written, (and, indeed, several have been—see p. 102). The Oregon Agate and Mineral Society of Portland publish a good map, pin-pointing the best collecting areas and describing the material available on each site. Many other states do the same.

OREGON

Over fifty percent of the land in Oregon is state-owned, but other areas require a collecting fee.

The Carey Ranch, near Eagle Rock, south of Princeville, produces some superb plume agate (collecting fee). The triangular area bounded by the towns John Day, Burns and Bend, is the most productive field for plume agate, petrified wood and thunder eggs, while agates occur at many places along the Pacific coast down to the Californian border. In the vicinity of Sucker Creek in the Malheur County, moss agate, jasper and petrified wood are found in the rim rocks and in the beds of creeks.

Some of the county's best petrified wood is found at Nigger Rock and also at Sucker Creek – whole trees are buried a few feet down under gravel conglomerate. In eastern Oregon in Baker county, some very good gem agates are found and at Shirtail Creek some equally fine dark green jasper.

On the Californian border in the Jackson county, Melford provides a good headquarters for the various expeditions into the surrounding areas. At Eagle Point, north-west of Medford on Highway 62, good carnelian and moss agate occur and very fine quartz crystals may be gathered on the heights above McCloud on Crater Lake Highway, some of them exceedingly long. This whole area is very good collecting country, and in the adjoining county of Douglas, agate, iris agate, carnelian, jasper and bloodstone are found in company with several other gemstones.

Along the Pacific shores of Oregon, collecting is most rewarding. Walking down these beaches, practically every wave washes up some interesting stone, the best time being just after the winter storms when the uppermost layer of pebbles is skimmed away revealing precious material that may have been long buried. In this wet state it is easy to see the prize specimens.

The northern stretches provide some jasper of the bloodstone variety. The famous Agate Beach furnishes the finest varieties of these, although they are usually small.

Collecting areas for many other gemstones in Oregon are: on the borders of Idaho, also the boundary of Morrow and Gilliam Counties – good opal and quartz. Obsidian is found in North East Lake, and some garnet occurs on the Californian border here.

CALIFORNIA

California provides an abundance of rich mineral material, both in the desert and along the coast. Almost forty-five percent of the state is owned by the us Government, and includes four National Parks where 'rock hunting' is not permitted. The booklet *Californian Gem Trails* should be studied for detailed information about this state, as only a very general survey can be made here.

The three mountain ranges in north-east Imperial county and in Riverside county to the north, are vast reservoirs of quartz gemstones of every variety, while just over the northern border of Imperial county, Little Chocolate Mountains are renowned for their fine large geodes lined with amethyst crystals and also clear quartz ones, many of which have chalcedony-filled centres glowing with colour.

The well-known fire agate comes from this area. When it has been carefully ground, it reveals all the colours of the rainbow and has an iridescent flash, resembling an opal. These agates cannot be subjected to the conventional cutting and polishing, as the inclusions which cause the fire are near the surface and may vanish while the stone is being worked.

The equally famous Hauser Geode beds lie beyond Coon Hollow Road on the Black Hills Road, south of Highway 60–70. This is probably one of the greatest collecting areas in the United States, and many enthusiasts are always found working here. A general area, known as the Wiley Well district, provides almost every type of chalcedony and agate that is found elsewhere in the States.

Another important county for the gem collector is San Diego, where minerals occurring in the pegmatite group are: aquamarine, tourmaline, topaz, garnet, kunzite, rose and clear quartz, although many of these are found in privately-owned mines.

In San Bernardino county, the Barstow vicinity of the Mojave Desert is also a good collecting area where you could spend a week or two, accumulating quartz finds every day. On Calico Mountains to the north of Highway 91, and adjacent to the city of Barstow, mineral specimens in rich variety may be gathered. Petrified palm root, one of the most remarkable types of petrified wood for polishing, is also found in this area – when cut into cabochons very unusual rings may be made.

The beautiful Red Rock Canyon, structured in ancient eroded canyons of brilliant red, are not only a scenic experience but are filled with an array of many different gemstones, which include opal and agate. Other areas that are outstanding and should be mentioned are – Nipomo, four miles north of Santa Maria, prolific in rare and beautiful agates, but seldom accessible, (though they may sometimes be bought from local farmers), and Stone Canyon, near San Miguel, now privately-owned but providing some of the finest jasper in the country.

A rewarding coastal stretch for collecting runs north of San Francisco and is especially good in the Crescent City area. Similar agates to those found on the Oregon beaches are here, and although less plentiful they are of a fascinating lemon colour. Jasper and agatized wood should also be plentiful from time to time.

While these two states, Oregon and California, are probably the most productive areas in the country, most other states have rich mineral deposits, and many fine varieties are available in Canada – Labradorite occurring extensively in the vicinity of Nairn and Paul Islands, moonstone from Lyndhurst, Ontario, while the Petrified Forest National Monument in Arizona is one of the most astonishing and spectacular sights and should certainly be visited. Although these petrified forests are now protected by legislation and stringent rules are in force against the removal of specimens, they are a phenomenon that should not be missed.

Other localities

Rough minerals sold by suppliers come from many parts of the world, some countries being famous for certain gemstones.

BRAZIL
Adventurine, chrysoprase, rose quartz, agate varieties, amethyst, most quartz varieties, citrine, aquamarine

AUSTRALIA
Opal, amethyst, rhodonite, lace agate, ribbonstone, beryl, aquamarine, garnet

SOUTHERN AFRICA
Tiger eye, blue lace agate, malachite (katanga), beryl, amazonite, moonstone, green garnet, desert rose, topaz, tourmaline, red jasper

AFGHANISTAN
Lapis lazuli

GERMANY (IDAR OBERSTEIN)
Agate, main market for world-wide gemstones

PERSIA
Turquoise

MEXICO
Opal, obsidian, agate varieties, calcite

CHILE
Pale blue lapis lazuli

CEYLON
Chrysoberyl, tourmaline, zircon

Many other countries export precious and semi-precious stones and you should gain experience by buying the varieties in the form of rough in the first stages. Dealers will usually supply this on a sale or return basis. However, it is always best to choose your material personally whenever possible.

List of suppliers

British Isles

LAPIDARY MACHINES AND SUPPLIES

M. L. Beach, 41 Church Street, Twickenham, Middlesex (Lapidary machines, tumblers, grits, rough and tumbled minerals)

Gemstones, 35 Princes Avenue, Hull, Yorkshire (Lapidary machines, tumblers and lapidary supplies)

Ammonite Ltd, Llandow Industrial Estate, Cowbridge, Glamorgan (All lapidary equipment and supplies)

Glenjoy Lapidary Supplies, 89 Westgate, Wakefield, Yorkshire (Lapidary equipment and supplies)

Gemrocks, 7/8 High Holborn, London EC1 (Lapidary equipment, supplies, books)

Wessex Gems and Crafts Ltd, Lanham Lane, Winchester, Hampshire (Lapidary machines, equipment and supplies)

Hirsh Jacobson Ltd, 91 Marylebone High Street, London W1 (Lapidary machines)

Kernocraft Rocks and Gems, 44 Lemon Street, Truro, Cornwall (Lapidary equipment and supplies)

Whitear Lapidary Co., 35 Ballards Lane, London N3 (Lapidary machines and equipment)

P.M.R. Lapidary Equipment, Pitlochry, Perthshire, Scotland (Lapidary machines, equipment, books)

A. and D. Hughes Ltd, Pope's Lane, Oldbury, Warley, Worcestershire (Lapidary machines and combination units)

SUPPLIERS OF MATERIALS

Bezalel Gems Co., 67/68 Hatton Garden, London EC1 (Cut slabs and rough specimens of precious and semi-precious stones)

Pebblegems, 41 King James Avenue, Cuffley, Potters Bar, Hertfordshire (Rough and tumbled stones, grits and polishes)

Lythe Minerals, 36 Oxford Street, Leicester (Good range of material)

Keystones, 1 Local Board Road, Watford, Hertfordshire (Most supplies)

The Stone Corner, 242 St Helen's Road, Hastings, Sussex (Good selection of cutting material and specimens)

The Rockhound Shop, 66 Front Street, Newbiggin by the Sea, Northumberland (Rough material)

R. Lane, 10 Beach Road, Perranporth, Cornwall (Tumble mixes, pebbles, grits)

R. F. D. Parkinson and Co. Ltd, Doulting, Shepton Mallet, Somerset (Minerals and cutting material)

Saundry, Chapel Street, Penzance, Cornwall (Minerals, machines, maps, books, findings)

Love-rocks, 56/58 North Street, Bedminster, Bristol 8 (Tumbling mixes, rough rocks for tumbling and cabochons)

Stones and Settings, 54 Main Street, Prestwick, Scotland (Interesting tumble mixes of semi-precious material)

George Stanley and Co., Natural Science Laboratories, Bwichgwyn Quarry, Wrexham, Denbyshire (Suppliers of geological specimens)

Alvi Gems, 313 Keal Drive, Glasgow W5 (Suppliers of jewelry findings)

Peak Minerals, 11 Borrowell, Kegworth, Derby (Collectors' specimens, opal chips, lapidary supplies)

Overseas

W. Martin Blum, P.O. Box 1974, Sao Paulo, Brazil (Tumbling rough, cutting material, specimens)

Parasmani Trading Co., 8 Warden Court, Gowalia Tank, Bombay 26, India (Rough and cut semi-precious stones)

Queensland Opal Cutters, P.O. Box 154, Gladstone, Queensland, Australia (All grades of opals, samples and price lists supplied)

Australian Gem Trading Co., 294 Little Collins Street, Melbourne, Australia (Opal suppliers, specializing in direct buying by mail)

Minex Lapidary Supplies Pty Ltd, 306 Russell Street, Melbourne, Australia (Suppliers of lapidary equipment, semi-precious, rough)

D. F. Roder, Box 77, Andamooka Opal Fields, S. Australia (Selected opal pieces, graded slabbed opal for cabochons)

Gemstones, P.O. Box 133, Pofadder, Via Kakamas, S. Africa (Exporters of tiger eye)

Albert Leyser, D 638 Fischbach/Nahe, Idar Oberstein, Germany (Suppliers of rough gemstones, polished eggs and balls)

Geo Rock Shop, Marcello de Alvear, 628 Local 14, Buenos Aires, Argentine (Suppliers of Chilean lapis lazuli)

Hugo Becker, E.C. Hauptstrasse 52, Idar Oberstein, Germany (Suppliers)

Ernst Winter & Sohn, Osterstrasse 58, Hamburg 19, Germany (Suppliers)

Wilhelm Danner, Schalhouser Strasse 98, Nuremberg 34, Germany (Suppliers)

PUBLICATIONS

Lapidary Journal, P.O. Box 2369, San Diego, California 92112, USA

Gems, The British Lapidary Magazine, 29 Ludgate Hill, London EC4

Suppliers in United States

MK Diamond Products, Highland Park Manufacturing, 12600 Chadron Avenue, Hawthrone, California 90250 (Suppliers of some of the finest lapidary equipment)

Brad's Rock Shop, 911 W. Nine Mile Road, Ferndale (Detroit), Michigan 48220 (Lapidary equipment and materials)

Aspen Lapidary. Showroom: 4815 E. 48 Avenue, Denver, Colorado. Mailing address: P.O. Box 1558, Denver, Colorado (Mineral supplies from S. Africa, India, Brazil, S.W. Africa)

3 M Company, Building 224–55, 3 M Centre, St Paul, Minnesota 55101 (Lapidary machines, diamond blades, discs, belts, grits)

Scott-Murray Mfg. Co., Box 25077, Northgate Station, Seattle, Washington 98125 (Excellent six-sided all-rubber tumblers and tumbling materials)

Lortons Inc., 2854 N.W. Market Street, Seattle, Washington 98107 (Slab and trim saws)

Nogalee Manufacturing Co., 435 Grand Avenue, Nogalee, Arizona 85021 (Producers of automatic cabochon grinder)

Shipley's Mineral House, Gem Village, Bayfield, Colorado 81122 (Suppliers of all lapidary equipment and materials)

Estwing Mfg Co., Dept. L. J. 11, 2647 8th Street, Rockford, Illinois 61101 (Suppliers of collectors' tools, picks, hammers, chisels, etc.)

Murray American Corporation, 15 Commerce Street, Chatham, N.J. 07928 (Tumbling materials)

Ace Lapidary Supply, 6015 Sepulvedo Blvd, Van Nuys, California (Custom slabbing and polishing, all supplies)

Aleta's Rock Shop, 1515 Plainfield, N.E. Grand Rapids, Michigan 49505 (Tumbling and cutting material, grits, polishing powders)

Allen Lapidary Equipment Manufacturing Co., P.O. Box 75411, Oklahoma City, Oklahoma 73107 (Cabochon combination machines)

Ammolite Minerals Ltd, 4703 Waverley Drive, Calgary 5, Alberta, Canada (Ammolite and other mineral rough)

A. L. Greer, Milky Ranch, Box 145 Holbrook, Arizona (Phone 524.3237) (Collecting area for petrified wood, campers welcomed, slabs supplied)

Apache Tear Caves, Box 7, Superior, Arizona (Cave visiting and collecting permitted)

William Munz, P.O. Box 639, Nome, Alaska 99762 (Supplies of Alaska nephrite jade)

Fundy Rocks and Minerals, RR 3 St Stephen, New Brunswick, Canada (Cabochon slabs in agate and other minerals)

Geode Industries, 106–108 W. Main, U.S. Highway 34, New London, Iowa (agencies in England) (Vibratory tumblers and lapidary equipment)

Bibliography

A field guide to rocks and minerals by Frederick H. Pough. Ed. R. T. Peterson. Lapidary Journal Book Department, USA 1970

Agates by Lelande Quick. Pitman and Sons, London; Chilton Book Company, Philadelphia 1963

An introduction to minerals by J. Ladurner and F. Purtcheller. Pinguin Verlag, Innsbruck

An introduction to the mineral kindom by Richard H. Pearl. Blandford Press, London 1966

British regional geology guides. HM Stationery Office, London

Collecting and polishing stones by Herbert Scarfe. Batsford, London 1970

Collecting gems and decorative stones by Kenneth Blakemore and Gordon Andrews. Foyles, London

Collector's guide to minerals and gemstones by Hellmuth Boegel. Thames and Hudson, London: Viking Press Inc., New York (as *The Studio handbook of minerals*) 1972

Dana's textbook of mineralogy. Chapman and Hall, London 1949; John Wiley and Sons Inc., New York, 4th edition 1932

Gem cutting, a lapidary manual by John Sinkankas. D. Van Nostrand and Co. Inc., Princetown, New Jersey 1962

Gem tumbling and baroque jewellery making by Victors. Victor Agate shop, California USA

Gems, their sources, descriptions and identification by Robert Webster. NAG Press, London EC4

Gemcraft by Lelande Quick and Hugh Leiper. Pitman and Sons, London; Chilton Book Company, Philadelphia 1959

Gemmologists' Compendium by Robert Webster. NAG Press, London EC4, 1947

Gemstones by G. E. Herbert Smith. Methuen, London 1912

Gemstones and minerals, how and where to find them by John Sinkankas. D. Van Nostrand and Co. Inc., Princetown, New Jersey 1961

Gemstones of North America by John Sinkankas. D. Van Nostrand and Co. Inc., Princetown, New Jersey 1959

Geology and scenery in Britain by T. G. Miller. Batsford, London 1953

Geology for schools by J. T. Greensmith. Leonard Hill, London 1964

Guide to collection of gemstones in the geological museum by W. F. B. McLintock. HM Stationery Office, London 1963

Knaurs miniralien buch by Hellmuth Boegel. Droemer Knaur, Munich-Zurich 1968

Minerals and man by Cornelius S. Hurlbut Jnr. Thames and Hudson, London 1969; Random House, New York 1968

Minerals and mineral deposits by W. R. Jones and D. Williams. Oxford University Press, London 1949

Minerals and rocks in colour by J. F. Kirkaldy. Blandford Press, London 1963

Minerals, rocks and gemstones in Cornwall and Devon by Cedric Rogers. D. Bradford Barton Ltd, Devon 1968

Observer's book of British geology by I. O. Evans. Frederick Warne and Co. Ltd, London 1949

Popular gemology by Richard H. Pearl. Sage Books, New York 1965

Practical gemology by Robert Webster. NAG Press, London 1952; Wehman Brothers, Hackenack, New Jersey

Precious stones by Max Bauer. Charles Griffin and Co., London 1904

Precious stones and minerals by Dr Herman Bank. Frederick Warne, London 1970

Precious stones and other crystals by R. Metz. Lapidary Journal Book Department, USA 1964

Principles of physical geology by Arther Holmes. Nelson, London 1944; The Ronald Press Co., New York 1965

Rocks and minerals by Herbert Zim and Paul Shaffer. Paul Hamlyn, London 1965; Golden Press, Western Publishing Co., Racine, Wisconsin 1957

The art of the lapidary by Francis J. Sperisen; Bruce Publishing Co., Milwaukee, Wisconsin, revised 1961

The amateur geologist by Peter Cattermole; Butterworth, London 1968

The face of the earth by G. H. Drury. Pelican Books, London 1959

The mineral kingdom by Paul E. Desautels

The pebbles on the beach by Clarence Ellis. Faber, London 1965

The sea coast by J. A. Steers, Collins, London 1969

The story of gems and semi-precious stones by Frederick H. Pough. Lapidary Journal Book Department

Tumblers guide by Balej

Index

(*Numbers in italics at end of entries refer to figure numbers*)